ACHIEVING LONGEVITY

How Great Firms Prosper
through Entrepreneurial Thinking

ACHIEVING LONGEVITY

How Great Firms Prosper
through Entrepreneurial Thinking

JIM DEWALD

UNIVERSITY OF TORONTO PRESS
Toronto Buffalo London

© University of Toronto Press 2016
Rotman-UTP Publishing
Toronto Buffalo London
www.utppublishing.com
Printed in Canada

ISBN 978-1-4426-5029-9

∞ Printed on acid-free, 100% post-consumer recycled paper with vegetable-based inks.

Library and Archives Canada Cataloguing in Publication

Dewald, Jim, 1956–, author
Achieving longevity : how great firms prosper through entrepreneurial thinking/Jim Dewald.

Includes bibliographical references and index.
ISBN 978-1-4426-5029-9 (cloth)

1. Creative ability in business.   2. Decision making.   3. Entrepreneurship – Psychological aspects.   4. Industrial management.   I. Title.

HD53.D49 2016   658.4'063   C2016-901011-2

University of Toronto Press acknowledges the financial assistance to its publishing program of the Canada Council for the Arts and the Ontario Arts Council, an agency of the Government of Ontario.

Canada Council Conseil des Arts
for the Arts du Canada

Funded by the   Financé par le
Government   gouvernement
of Canada   du Canada

Canada

ONTARIO ARTS COUNCIL
CONSEIL DES ARTS DE L'ONTARIO
an Ontario government agency
un organisme du gouvernement de l'Ontario

CONTENTS

FOREWORD

One of the best personal decisions I ever made was to pursue an MBA degree in entrepreneurship. I was about graduate number 225 from the University of Calgary's total MBA program, and – to my knowledge – the first to graduate with a major in entrepreneurship. At that time, entrepreneurship was a fledgling area of study, one that wasn't well respected or even clearly understood – kind of like the black sheep of business schools. Entrepreneurs were people you saw in movies. Studying entrepreneurship wasn't part of a serious business career in accounting or finance – and especially in investment banking.

Several decades later, entrepreneurship is one of the most celebrated topics in the world of business, and even around the kitchen table. Shows like *Dragons' Den* are favourites of parents *and* their children, for they're planting seeds with a new generation of people who, regardless of their vocation, education, race, religion, or even age, believe that they too could be in business for themselves someday. This entrepreneurial revival is important for the future of Canada as it offers inspiration for anyone who wants to be part of bringing innovation to life, driving economic growth, and enhancing our communities.

Unfortunately, the entrepreneurial mindset is often apparently confined to the ranks of the supposed renegades and risk takers who are willing to step out and bet the farm on a new idea. That prevailing attitude is part of the problem. Society tends to think that entrepreneurs are people who graduate from business schools. And academia normally links entrepreneurial studies with small business. On both counts, I couldn't disagree more. Along with marketing and philanthropy, entrepreneurship is something *everyone* should study for life. In fact, I would argue that these three subjects should be core curriculum for students starting as early as grade three and continuing right through all forms of advanced education – be it vocational school, college, or university.

Entrepreneurship is way of thinking. It's about innovation. And if there is one lesson I've learned from my career, it's that anyone, anywhere, can have/develop/enjoy an entrepreneurial mindset. Whether you're an employee or an employer, an artist, a welder, or an accountant, you can find ways to innovate and be part of the creative process. Innovative thinkers are constantly asking one simple question: "How can we make things better?"

Since graduating with my MBA more than three decades ago, supporting entrepreneurship has been an ongoing passion of mine. I enjoyed three seasons on *Dragons' Den* and have invested in and mentored more than thirty businesses from the show in the years since. I travel the country with a steady schedule of talks to business and student audiences. A key initiative was funding the Wilson Centre for Entrepreneurial Excellence at the University of Saskatchewan, whose mandate is to foster and inspire entrepreneurial thinking in *all* colleges, regardless of discipline. The centre teaches people from multiple disciplines and generations how to try out innovation in low-risk settings, and to transfer that learning into the corporate world.

My life journey of discovering my inner passion and skills as an entrepreneur is why I wholeheartedly recommend this book about how to achieve corporate longevity by reigniting an entrepreneurial mindset within corporate culture. Jim expands on our collective understanding of the value of entrepreneurial thinking for society, and he helps us understand *how* – and equally importantly, *why* – to apply that thinking in the corporate world. He rightly points out that the corporate community is crowded with people who unfortunately have lost their natural intuition to be entrepreneurial. Their primary focus is often more on efficiency rather than innovation; on avoiding risk rather than embracing opportunity; and on safely following competitors rather than blazing their own trail.

Jim argues that the same interest in entrepreneurship that is being generated in classrooms, conference rooms, and living rooms is desperately needed in boardrooms. He clearly illustrates the long-term positive impact of a corporate culture that encourages and enables everyone from the reception desk to the C-suite to engage in entrepreneurial thinking. His fascinating and actionable insights into *how* to enable that culture – and the pitfalls and barriers that can impede the way – are invaluable for any corporate leader who wants to reach beyond the status quo.

Jim's book is a call to action to corporate leaders to quit defending the old ways, and to instead focus on how to use their sizable resources, capabilities, processes, and networks to change for the better. For any business person who pursues longevity (and most of us do), Jim provides the honest truth: being too rigid will break you, while being agile (and taking decisive action) is the only real competitive advantage we have. Entrepreneurial thinking breeds agility; it makes firms more innovative, more adaptive to changing markets and technology, more responsive to community needs, and better able to survive (and thrive) over the long term. One sector that could benefit from an even more entrepreneurial mindset is Canada's own energy industry – an industry already rich with a tradition of innovation that we need to renew and invigorate.

Jim's case is so compelling you'll wonder why anyone would build a business that *didn't* inspire entrepreneurship and innovation at every level. Beyond helping achieve longevity, entrepreneurial thinking is *fun*! It lets people explore, be creative, take risks, partner with others, and, in the process, leave their companies – and the world – much better off. For those who wonder whether entrepreneurs are born or made, Jim's book confirms that the answer is – always – *yes!*

W. Brett Wilson
Entrepreneur, Philanthropist, Dragon Emeritus
October 2015

ACKNOWLEDGMENTS

A book project is a big commitment and requires the support of many people. I want to start by thanking my family for their steadfast support – my wife Chris, son Matt, daughter Danya, and father Henry.

Being a dean is quite a busy job, and I am very sure I would have never taken on this challenge without the support and encouragement of Professor Alain Verbeke. Alain has consistently provided me with tremendous mentorship and guidance, always honest and always valuable. Thank you so much.

In addition to the tremendous support and insight I received from the team at the University of Toronto Press (thank you UTP team!), Mike Heffring provided very important guidance, indeed redirection after reviewing an early version of the manuscript. I also received excellent and valuable insights through early reviews and comments from Lesley Conway, Peter Tertzakian, Mac Van Wielingen, and Brett Wilson. Thank you for your important contributions.

Jason Hardy and the specialized team at Chatterson Drive provided invaluable support, advice, and graphical expertise. This included designing the cover and all of the figures for the book. Thank you so much.

I am blessed with an amazing team at the Haskayne School of Business and have many people to thank for their support and guidance. In particular, I want to note the pioneering work from the team at the Hunter Centre for Entrepreneurship and Innovation, including Director Kim Neutens, RBC Teaching Professor Derek Hassay, Elizabeth Allen, Kevan Coyle, Houston Peschl, and Bob Schulz. This exceptional team benefits from the guidance of a blue-ribbon advisory panel that includes Doug and Derrick Hunter, Wayne Henuset, Keith Brown, Jeff Boyd, Dave and Jeff Robson, and Charlie Locke.

The leadership team at the Haskayne School of Business is always supportive, and for this project I received tremendous help from Loren Falkenberg, Kim Kadatz, Vern Jones, Sherry Weaver, Scott Radford, Michael Wright, Krista Larson, and Bree Austen. Implementing the craft of entrepreneurial thinking requires advanced leadership skills, which are the purview of the Canadian Centre for Advanced Leadership in Business, led by Jenny Krahn, Piers Steel, and Stella George.

I also want to acknowledge Sumeet Mehta, recent MBA graduate and research assistant on the project.

ACHIEVING LONGEVITY

How Great Firms Prosper
through Entrepreneurial Thinking

Introduction

I needed to write this book because I am concerned that businesses in general, and business leaders in particular, have lost touch with the all-important entrepreneurial spirit that drove growth and prosperity in the past. In a mature economic system such as what we have in North America, business leaders have lost the hunger to be entrepreneurial and corporations have instead chosen to follow one another. This is not only accepted practice, but also encouraged through management theory and investor demands.

There are enticing benefits to being a corporate follower, at least in the short term. Following can minimize risk and provide a certain level of comfort and reliability, as well as the perception of safe and secure markets and prosperity. However, the evidence does not support this vision, particularly in the long term. A bigger concern is that as business leaders slowly move into misguided illusions of comfortable returns, they move closer to being ill-prepared should real change hit them.

Well, you may be asking, "What is real change if it is not what we are experiencing today?" Sure, your latest iPhone may have new features, and the latest social media craze may be preoccupying your time, but from a historic standpoint, we are not experiencing fundamental change, the kind of change that impacts how we live our daily lives. The last real period of change occurred between sixty and a hundred years ago, and it resulted in a one-time quantum shift brought about by the declining cost of transportation (through introduction of the automobile, the airplane, and the telephone) and the ubiquitous convenience of a plug-in world (through electric wiring to homes and places of work). These changes drove economic growth in the twentieth century, but that engine is wearing out. We may perceive massive and rapid change today, but our perspective is relative. What strikes us as changes are actually shifts toward greater efficiency, exploitation, and commoditization. This context, which will be described more fully in chapter 1, defines where we have been and where we are heading (barring an intervention such as a proliferation of entrepreneurial thinking).

On the corporate side, I have dealt with hundreds of chief executive officers, and what I see is that more than anything, they seek to lead their organizations toward sustainability and to leave a legacy or platform for success that will live on long after they have retired. They seek longevity. Yet the evidence shows that longevity is actually very rare. I will provide evidence in chapter 3 that the life span of most corporations is a mere fraction of the average person's work life. This presents a stark contrast to the desires of corporate leaders. Why is this so, and what can be done to reverse this?

When conceiving this book, I wanted to better understand how organizations achieve longevity, the kind of longevity that survives long past the founder or any particular leader or leadership team. Professors of business and corporate strategy (which includes me) research and lecture about the goal of long-term "sustained" competitive advantage, driven by grand plans and sub-strategies that mesmerize and seduce the most seasoned leaders and leadership teams. Unfortunately, on reflection I find that I don't necessarily buy the construct of sustainable competitive advantage beyond it being a useful concept for learning. The evidence does not support it as a path to longevity. Instead, what I have observed is that the seeds of longevity are found in entrepreneurial thinking and innovation – in exploring ways to adapt corporate and business strategies in response to market, technological, and social and cultural change.

There it is. The common view is that (1) the world is changing ever more rapidly (some say faster than ever before in history), and (2) the best way to achieve corporate longevity is through sustained competitive advantage. In contrast, I argue that (1) we are in a period of dangerously minimal change that is driving commoditization that rewards efficiency and cost reduction over innovation, and (2) organizations, whether faced by rapid or minimal change, achieve longevity through entrepreneurial thinking and capability development that rewards innovation.

In this book, I present detailed support of my argument, which ultimately supports the broader goal of achieving longevity. Some would contend that corporate longevity may not, on its own, be in society's best interests. In other words, are the biggest goals of our society best served by corporate longevity? That I don't know, and while this could be debated, I ask that you accept the altruism of individual leaders as they seek to achieve corporate longevity, which provides jobs, economic growth, and many other social and economic benefits.

Everyone Is Talking about Entrepreneurship

As a business school dean, I am exposed to most of the trends in curriculum development, and today the hottest topic in business schools is entrepreneurship. Every year there are masses of books published about entrepreneurship and related matters. "Pivot," "lean," "exponential," "just-in-time," and other catchphrases are being introduced into a new dialogue that encourages us to think of entrepreneurship as sexy. "Rags to riches" storytelling has even attracted Hollywood. I think this is great, and very energizing, but we need to be cautious: not every garage start-up turns into the next Google or Facebook. The odds are severely against that outcome.

At the same time, I have to acknowledge that at least in academe, our understanding of entrepreneurship has progressed significantly. Most books, theories, and courses about entrepreneurship no longer focus on unreliable guesstimates; we no longer try to identify some rare mix of individual character traits as the path to entrepreneurial success. The idea that to be a successful entrepreneur, a person must be bold, gregarious, and self-centered may make for good fiction, but it does not stand up to empirical, evidence-based research.

Caution is in order: many authors seem determined to provide the perfect "formula" for success – "do this, then do that, and presto, you're rich." This trend is somewhat disturbing, because it replaces one mistaken theory (that only certain personalities will succeed as entrepreneurs) with another (that there is a magic formula that guarantees success). The reality is that, like other human phenomena, entrepreneurship is complex and uncertain and requires creativity, vast knowledge, agility, adaptability, judgment, action-orientation, an ability to make the right moves at the right time, guts, and a bit of luck. I am sorry to say that if you were hoping for a three-step get-rich-quick formula, you are reading the wrong book.

Success comes from having the right direction and purpose, from never shying away from hard work, and from consistently channeled effort. No two organizations are exactly alike, and my goal is to provide a constructive framework that can be adapted and shaped to fit any given organization's uniqueness. Longevity is a result of connecting the unique strengths of each organization with the right opportunities in the marketplace, and being able to adapt to meet market conditions as they change. Through careful study of many firms that have achieved longevity, as well as primary research on decision-making behavior and motivation theory, I have developed a framework to help organizations identify and develop their own unique paths to longevity. I will be presenting that framework here.

To make the topic even more alluring, consider that the long-term survival of a firm – say, over several generations, perhaps even more than a century – does not depend on some specific hard-to-find sustained competitive advantage, but rather on the firm's ability to engage corporate entrepreneurship as a means to adapt to changing markets, technologies, and/or social-cultural factors. To survive, firms need to be agile. This may reflect evolutionary theory, I'm not sure, but it is certainly observable in great companies.

So this book focuses mainly on corporate entrepreneurship. I find it fascinating that corporations are inherently capable and sufficiently resourced to succeed in entrepreneurial ventures – they have the money, the ideas, the brainpower, the leadership capabilities, the sales channels, the suppliers, the research facilities, the customers, the status, and so on. In short, existing corporations already have almost everything an individual entrepreneur seeks in the pursuit of success. So why isn't there more corporate entrepreneurship? It is because corporate entrepreneurs face institutional barriers, which include rigid strategic plans, risk-adverse decision-making processes, rules that restrict behaviors, and a low tolerance for failure both within the firm and within society. Organizations have the capabilities and resources, but they lack the processes necessary for corporate entrepreneurship. This can be fixed.

The stakes are high, for there is very low tolerance in the marketplace for firms that experiment with new ideas that fail. The individual entrepreneur is expected to fail, whereas the corporation is expected to be stable and to grow steadily to the next level, and the next level, and so on.

In this book I explore and address three distinct questions:

1 What is driving the renewed interest in entrepreneurship – specifically, corporate entrepreneurship? Are we entering a new era in which corporate entrepreneurship will become essential, even for short-term success?
2 How can existing business firms best prepare themselves to be entrepreneurial?
3 What are the pitfalls or barriers, and how can firms and managers best prepare for these unexpected concerns?

When we turn to history as a guide for where we are heading, we find that originally, business corporations were limited-term charters that focused on specific initiatives, such as the construction of a bridge, a dam, or a power plant. Astonishingly, the life span of business firms is even shorter today than it was under the original charters of the 1600s. Back then, laws were enacted to limit the life span of firms; today, market forces are limiting those life spans even further.

A large contributor to the rapid failure of firms is the drive for efficiency – a drive that has been institutionalized to such an extent that most business leaders are not even aware of the macro-scale shift. Only by stepping back and studying our economic transformation over the past 125 years can we see where we are headed (see chapter 1). Will a continued drive for efficiency be addressed through economies of scale and fewer and fewer, larger and larger firms? Or are we in the midst of a cycle where, through research and education, we are finding more sustainable ways – such as developing the capability to engage entrepreneurial thinking – for firms to achieve longevity? While I can't answer those questions, I will be providing evidence in this book that if we remain on our current trajectory, the drive for more and more efficiency may eventually spell ruin for most individual business firms. More specifically, it is easy to argue that today, a business firm that does nothing more than try to match its competition faces certain ruin. That is why I feel this topic is of critical importance to anyone in a leadership or managerial position in business.

Let me be even more direct and spell out the feedback cycle that has led to a shift away from agile entrepreneurship toward rigid strategic planning and the consequent need for more entrepreneurial thinking (points that will be reviewed in more detail later in the book):

- Problem 1 – **Managers follow their competitors**. They do this because it is endorsed and rewarded by analysts, financiers, and shareholders. It is even researched and taught in business school.[1]
- Problem 2 – **Firms fail**. They do so partly because they follow one another and hence find it difficult to change when market, technological, or economic conditions change.
- Problem 3 – **Management research and education is based on observations**. This means that over time, education cycles through problems 1 through 3, in a race to the bottom.[2]

To make matters worse, because of the unwavering focus on efficiency over the past century, business leaders have stripped away excess resources. This has reduced or eliminated the capacity of firms to innovate and to adapt to change. Through cost-cutting, firms have weeded out the learning or enacting of entrepreneurial skills, banking instead on the Holy Grail of sustainable competitive advantage as they search for core capabilities, valuable and rare resources, hedgehog concepts, and so on. The drive for resource-based advantage has been profitable, but it is always temporary, never permanent.

To be fair, leaders do grasp that some amount of change is inevitable; they recognize that the competitive environment changes as market needs change, technologies change, and cultural and societal values change. But I emphasize: sticking to a perceived sustained competitive resource-based advantage can lead to only one conclusion – failure, brought about by the inability to adapt effectively.

To achieve longevity and adapt to changing environments, business firms need to embrace entrepreneurial thinking, an entrepreneurial culture, and strategic entrepreneurship. This book presents a comprehensive view of the challenges noted above; it also calls for entrepreneurial thinking as the foundation for greater longevity and success. Figure I.1 illustrates the alternative paths – rigid strategic planning, or agile strategic entrepreneurship.

To keep on track with where we are heading, I will be referring to this figure (later labeled Figure 2.1) throughout the book. It is a simplification of the choice facing leaders, but it is helpful and instructive in understanding the potentially stark contrast between adopting a platform of strategic planning versus a platform of strategic entrepreneurship. This figure will be described in detail in chapter 2, but to provide an overview, its left-hand side shows the strategic management model that is provided in business school and is faithfully applied to almost all organizations, be they for-profit or not-for-profit. The objective is to seek strategic fit by matching the organization's resources, capabilities, and processes with the economic, social-cultural, and technological opportunities and challenges of the external environment. This can be viewed as the "stock" – where the firm stands.

Figure I.1 A model of strategic paths (planning versus entrepreneurship)

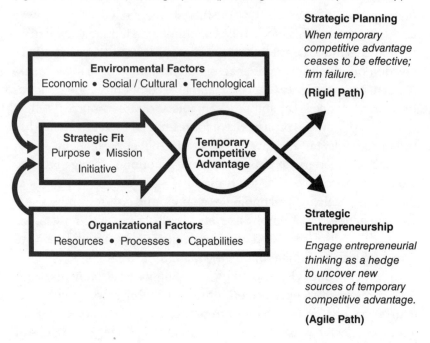

Strategic Planning

When temporary competitive advantage ceases to be effective; firm failure.

(Rigid Path)

Environmental Factors
Economic • Social / Cultural • Technological

Strategic Fit
Purpose • Mission
Initiative

Temporary Competitive Advantage

Organizational Factors
Resources • Processes • Capabilities

Strategic Entrepreneurship

Engage entrepreneurial thinking as a hedge to uncover new sources of temporary competitive advantage.

(Agile Path)

What is less discussed is the "flow" – that is, where the organization is going. This book focuses on the flow: Beyond finding strategic fit for today, how can the firm prepare itself to find the right strategic fit for the future? This is necessary if longevity is the goal.

My Story

I came to the realization that businesses need to be both stable and agile through a combination of my research (primarily on the impact of disruptive innovations on strategic decision-making), my teaching (most of which has been with experienced business leaders in executive education and MBA programs), and my own experience in the business world. My story in business and academe, which stretches back thirty-five years, is best described as unconventional. In fact, for my first forty-four years, it never occurred to me that I could or would be a professor, let alone the dean of a business school. But here I am, energized and at times overwhelmed by the challenge, yet excited about the difference we, business schools around the globe, are making in the lives of our students – the future leaders of our business community.

My path involved careers in engineering (where I rose to be a CEO and part-owner of a consulting practice), banking (where I learned how to finance large, complex projects), and real estate development (where, as a CEO of two major firms, I was able to stretch my creative side and experiment with various innovations – some that worked, some not so much). I entered a PhD program at forty-five and received my doctorate one month before turning fifty. From a business perspective, I had early successes; from an academic perspective, I would say I am still a work in progress.

Growing up in an entrepreneurial family shaped my sense of entrepreneurship. My father, partnering with his brother, started and operated his own construction business. In fact, all of my father's four brothers were self-employed like him, as were his three brothers-in-law. I think one of the main reasons why I succeeded in business was that as a result of this background, I never saw risks the same way others did. By and large, most people were not as excited as I was when it came to experimenting, to trying new ways to address changing consumer needs, to solving operational challenges. I have found that there are almost always new ways to tackle old problems. Consider this provocative passage from Nassim Nicholas Taleb, who quips about the struggles of carrying luggage through crowded airports in the mid-twentieth century:

> It struck me how lacking in imagination we are: we had been putting our suitcases on top of a cart with wheels, but nobody thought of putting tiny wheels directly under the suitcase. Can you imagine that it took close to six thousand years between the invention of the wheel

(by, we assume, the Mesopotamians) and this brilliant implementation
(by some luggage maker in a drab industrial suburb)?[3]

An example of small-scale innovation from my early days in real
estate development involves infrastructure installation in the form
of potable water and sewer utility pipelines. Real estate developers faced the recurring but costly and frustrating task of repairing
settled utility trenches that sank after a couple of years of freeze/
thaw cycles. This is a common problem in Canada, where winters
bring an abundance of snow and freezing temperatures. Over time,
everyone in the industry had just accepted the extra repair costs as
a necessary cost of doing business. In landscaped areas, we could
overfill trenches and easily dress up the settlement later, but most
utility lines were installed under paved roads, and even though the
contractors did their best to compact the soil, more often than not,
after two years there would be settlement, which meant tearing up
roads, recompacting the soil, and repaving the street. This was a
costly and inconvenient practice.

It was pointed out to me by one of our engineering consultants,
Harold Perrin, that when we placed larger volumes of soil in wide,
low-lying areas we did not face the same settlement problems. There
were two specific reasons for this: (1) the contractor could use larger, heavier compaction equipment to improve compaction in wider
zones, and (2) when clay fill was provided in broad areas, edge conditions were eliminated, and that is where differential settlement
occurred, causing much of the problem. This observation pointed
to a new, albeit more costly (up-front) solution – dig down, or leave
unfilled, approximately 1.5 meters for the entire street width rather
than the narrow trench areas, and use the heavier compaction equipment to intensify the compaction and eliminate the edge conditions
(which were prone to differential settlement). If the settlements were
not reduced, the company would be faced with an extra cost up-
front – the reduced settlement benefit was necessary to make the extra cost worthwhile.

I reported to an experienced and well-respected leader in the industry, David Harvie, who was open-minded and thus supportive. So we invested in the innovation. Our firm, Carma Developers, did face an up-front cost increase – I recall something in the 3 to 5 percent range. But after a couple of winters, we achieved a huge saving – around 50 percent of the post-construction maintenance and repair bill. The practice is now standard in the industry and has been extended to wider utility trenches that accommodate all underground utilities and service connections in one wider excavation, rather than the "old school" method of several narrow trenches, one for each utility mainline and service connection.

When I think back on that success, I recognize that Harold, the engineering consultant, was relaying an idea that had been conceived years earlier by a progressive contractor, Borger Construction. But because it was new and unproven and required up-front additional costs, none of his clients were willing to push the go button. They saw the risk if it did not work, yet the real risk was in *not* adopting a practice that could provide competitive advantage. I learned later that one of our competitors had also taken the initiative, spurred on by another engineering consultant, Fred Battle. This experience and others have taught me that employees, whether managers or not, find considerable comfort and significantly less risk in following what their competition does rather than trying new approaches. Time and again this has proved true, even when the new approach would gain competitive advantage for the firm.

There is an entire body of research, known as institutional theory, that studies how firms mimic other firms. Among its findings: Many executive decisions are based on following competitors – most notably, industry leaders. Furthermore, a surprising number of key decisions related to organizational structure, accounting policies, environmental policies, distribution channels, pricing strategies, marketing, and even organizational cultures are driven largely by the concern of managers to be seen as legitimate in the eyes of their competitors. I have no issue with the researchers – in fact, their work is highly sophisticated and rigorous – but how discouraging is it for us to think that senior executives at large firms would base their strategic decisions on following their competitors? Is this not a sad statement on the status of business leadership?

By the way, before we go too far, I acknowledge that (1) innovation is not always the best move for a firm, and (2) there are many barriers to innovation (described later in this book). Unfortunately, over the years I succumbed to some of those barriers in trying to implement several of my own entrepreneurial initiatives.

Moving Forward

This book has three parts. In part 1, we explore the changing (or not so much changing) economic environment and the role of strategy and entrepreneurship in understanding firm longevity and firm failure. Chapter 1 describes the technological and market change we have experienced over the past century, as well as the impact that change, or the lack of change, has had on management education and reward systems.

In chapter 2, we focus more narrowly on the business firm, examining the links between strategy as a management tool, entrepreneurship as a cultural orientation and process, and longevity as an outcome. Part 1 concludes with observations from industry, as well as a more direct consideration of the near inevitability of failure for business firms. It seems that what we mostly see is the economic success of market systems; we tend not to notice that almost all individual firms fail quite rapidly.

Part 2 serves as a "deep dive" into strategic entrepreneurship and entrepreneurial thinking. Chapters 4 through 7 provide a comprehensive theoretical validation of the entrepreneurial thinking model, which is central to the thesis of this book. I then explore how modern organizations can adopt a more entrepreneurial approach to decision-making and strategy development. Chapter 4 provides a clearer understanding of the link between corporate entrepreneurship and longevity. We then examine the micro-foundations of entrepreneurial thinking, which includes an analysis of thinking models (chapter 5); and a motivational model for entrepreneurial thinking (chapter 6). Finally, chapter 7 provides a framework for the entrepreneurial organization.

Returning to observed examples from the past, part 3 – more specifically, chapter 8 – pulls together the theoretical frameworks of dual decision-making processes, entrepreneurial thinking, and strategic entrepreneurship to develop a construct that confirms how great firms achieve longevity. In chapter 9, I delve into the multiple hurdles and barriers that exist within many (indeed most) business firms, limiting their potential for corporate entrepreneurship. Every organization starts with baggage, and every customer has a perspective that can cause even the best ideas to stumble. Research shows that efforts to build strong corporations create defensive force fields around the very idea of new ventures. Managers must be aware of the seeds of resistance and be purposeful in addressing them.

I end this introduction with an overview: This book focuses on the linkages among entrepreneurial thinking (as a foundation), corporate entrepreneurship (as an action), strategic entrepreneurship (as a process), and longevity (as an outcome). I want to celebrate the power of entrepreneurship in a team setting, where people combine their passion to form organizations and work collaboratively to build a sustainable difference in the lives of others. In my mind, there is scarcely a nobler act than to work collaboratively toward entrepreneurial ends – to provide value and purpose in ways that positively impact other humans. Doing so gives meaning to life itself. This is why I am passionate about entrepreneurial thinking and the message of this book. I hope you will find it helpful on your own journey to bring value and meaning to others.

PART ONE

The Current State of the World and Corporate Longevity

1 Faster, Smaller, Cheaper: A Time of Great Change?

Someone born in 1860, who lived to be 70 years old, grew up in a world of horses for travel, candles for light, salting and canning for food preservation, and telegraphs for communication. The world of their passing had cars and airplanes, electric light and refrigerators, telephones, radio, and motion pictures... We find ourselves wondering why our present progress seems so paltry in comparison.

Mark Huberty[1]

Try this at your next speaking engagement: Begin by asking the audience, "Do you feel like things are changing faster than what you can keep up with? Do you feel that every time you turn around, something new has caught you off guard? Tell me this – do you feel the world is changing more quickly than ever in history? Hold up your hand (or applaud) if you feel this way."

When I set out this question, it engages the audience. They enthusiastically agree that change is all around us and that it is a full-time job just to keep up. We often romanticize about the twentieth century and the first part of the twenty-first being an era of change. But has it really been a period of change?

I challenge that notion: in fact, for the most part, the twentieth century was about what Jim Collins (in his best-selling book *Good to Great*) calls the "flywheel." We actually spent the better part of the last century, and the first part of this one, improving the efficiency of known products so as to protect the way we lived about sixty years ago. As Mark Huberty, of the Berkeley Roundtable on the International Economy, states in the quote captured above, "We find ourselves wondering why our present progress seems so paltry."

In the first half of the twentieth century, pundits and intellectuals alike touted the promise of great change, contending that our lifestyle would be transformed through shorter workweeks, more recreation and relationship building, less administration, and so on. Instead, it was – and today continues to be – a period focused on making products faster, smaller, cheaper, and more convenient, while essentially sticking with the same products and patterns of living, working, and relaxing.

Let me give you a quick comparison. When my grandfather's family moved from Kansas to Canada in the very early twentieth century, it was a harrowing trip by train, with a boxcar shared between family and farm animals. A fire was kept going to save the family and animals from freezing to death, and food was stored and provided by the most primitive means. Toilets – forget about it. The family traveled next by horse-drawn carriage to a homestead where they lived in a shed until they were able to build a house from scratch. Every day was a question of survival.

Move on just one generation: when my dad moved, or I moved, or my children moved, it was essentially the same program – moving vans with professional movers that we followed in our private automobile or on a commercial plane. For about seventy years, most of us have lived in a modern home with central heating, wired electrical service, private wired telephone service, and municipal services (roads, sidewalks, potable water, parks, schools, etc.). Not just in the cities, even in towns. My grandfather, over the course of his life, went from not knowing what a motorized vehicle is to seeing Boeing 737 jets (still the dominant commercial plane) flying in the sky, and people on the moon. Throughout my own life, we have traveled mostly by private automobile at roughly the same speed on largely the same roads, flown on commercial planes, lived in houses that are fully serviced, shopped at supermarkets, communicated by telephone, and so on. The difference is that my grandfather witnessed what I will describe as general purpose technology paradigm change in his lifetime, whereas I, and probably you, have not. Think about that as a contrast in change. It is profound and humbling.

To better understand what we have witnessed over the past century or so, I engage the following framework to describe the fundamental stages of change:

1 *General purpose technology*[2] (GPT). GPT is a term developed by economists that refers to pervasive technologies that provide a inventive platform for developing complementary innovations that enable change that will "interrupt and accelerate the normal march of economic progress."[3]
2 *GPT innovation.* This reflects second-order innovations, emanating from the institutionalization/legitimization of a GPT. GPT innovations may cascade over a period when spin-off inventions based on a GPT are shaped into complementary and further-order innovations of commercial and utility value for entrepreneurs, firms, and society.
3 *GPT democratization.* This represents a somewhat explosive growth period when innovations become accessible, even ubiquitous, for society at large.
4 *GPT exploitation.* During this period, democratized innovations are refined through efficiencies and enhancements (faster, smaller, more convenient).
5 *GPT commoditization.* The focus is now on cheaper offerings, reflecting the loss of unique value and reduction to basic utility.

This framework may look familiar because the inspiration has been somewhat drawn from the "S" curve or technology life cycle. However, its stages occur on a much grander scale. In comparison, the technology life cycle plots product sales volume against time and highlights the stages of invention (akin to GPT invention), which leads to replication and improvement (innovation), then maturity (democratization), stabilization (exploitation), and finally decline (commoditization).

Consistent with the definition of a GPT, I have considered this framework in assessing a certain class of inventions that have changed the world. LiveScience[4] has isolated the top ten inventions of all time. They include the wheel (3500 BC), the nail (about 2,000 years ago), the compass (ninth to eleventh century), and the printing press (1440). Think, only ten such inventions – these are the true game changers and paradigm shifters of all time.

It is fascinating to note that over all that history, the twentieth century is unique in that it was rocked by three major inventions from the late nineteenth century: the lightbulb, the telephone, and the internal combustion engine.

The lightbulb was the catalyst for the democratization and exploitation of electricity, which was the actual general purpose technology. Similarly, the telephone was the catalyst for telephone cable wiring to homes and businesses, which has had a profound influence on communications, including the Internet, television communications, and so on. The internal combustion engine, also a highly prolific GPT, radically changed human mobility. Each of these inventions led to significant innovation, democratization, and exploitation stages.

Figure 1.1 illustrates the adoption of electricity, telephone, and the automobile, providing a rudimentary illustration of the periods of innovation, democratization, exploitation, and commoditization throughout the twentieth century. It matters little whether we focus on electricity, telephone, or the automobile – the pattern is always much the same. The differences are muted compared to the similarities in the shape of each curve. The one distinction that stands out is the influence of the Second World War on slowing the democratization of both the telephone and the automobile, but otherwise, the patterns are nearly identical in timing and shape.

Just to be clear, invention and innovation are distinct terms in academic studies, whether economics, management, or technology based. *Invention* is the creation, recombination, or discovery of something

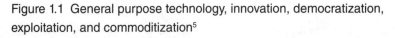

Figure 1.1 General purpose technology, innovation, democratization, exploitation, and commoditization[5]

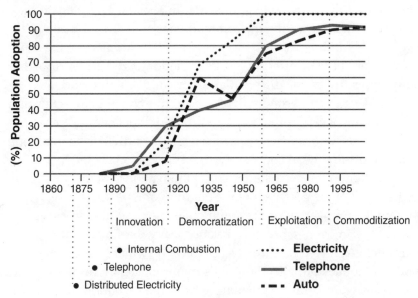

new. *Innovation* describes the initial commercialization of an invention. Consider a pharmaceutical drug. Penicillin is viewed as one of great medical inventions. The innovation of penicillin in antibiotics represented the commercialization of the invention. The invention of polymers led to the innovation of plastic containers and all sorts of other things, including synthetic clothing.

Democratization refers to the application, by entrepreneurs and managers, of economies of scale, scope, and learning to enhance the affordability and accessibility of products for a broader population. *Exploitation* refers to the continuous improvement of a product or service, which leads to faster, smaller, lighter, more convenient applications of the same service or product. Finally, during *commoditization*, products and services become much cheaper. As products and services lose their uniqueness, there begins a battle for the cheapest, or even for the disposable. Profits and financial margins are at their absolute thinnest during the commoditization stage, with allows for very little funding for further research or development of the product or service. The offering has been standardized and stripped of any opportunity for differentiation or unique value-add, leaving only efficiency and economies of scale to rule competitive action and strategy. A concern is that as a product moves deeper into commoditization, fewer resources are dedicated at the firm level to inventing and innovating what could be the next GPT.

To better understand the shift from innovation to democratization, let's consider the invention of the internal combustion engine, which led to the innovation of the automobile (along with many other innovations, most notably the airplane, heavy machinery, lawn mowers, etc.). At the turn of the twentieth century there were thousands of automobiles but also thousands of automakers. The automobile, a pervasive innovation emanating from the invention of the internal combustion engine, was a custom product available solely to the wealthiest in society. An exclusive product for an exclusive clientele represents innovation but not democratization. Then Henry Ford came along.

An interesting fact about Henry Ford is that he was on his third automobile venture before he found success with the Model T, which demonstrates the value of experimentation and learning from failure. Ford, who was brilliant at engineering and a passionate lover of speed, did not possess a formal degree in science, engineering, or management, but he realized better than all his competitors the benefits of standardization and economy-of-scale production. When he started his production line, the retail price of a car was roughly the same as the price of a home. Imagine today having to choose between a home and a car. Interestingly, the price of a small jet is nearing the price of a home – déjà vu?

Through mass production assembly line technology and the standardization of automobile features, in just a few years, Ford was able to reduce the price of a car to less than 20 percent of the price it was when he started production. This is a vivid example of how invention (the internal combustion engine) led to innovation (in the form of the motor vehicle), which then led to democratization as Henry Ford took an exclusive product and made it accessible to the common person.

Ford became an icon of business and economic prowess, proving that scientific management theory, mass production techniques, and standardized product design can result in high-quality products at a fraction of the customized alternative. Arguably, the technology behind assembly line manufacturing could be a contender as another general purpose technology, but let's not cloud the story too much. The necessary complement to the assembly line was product design standardization, best captured by Ford's famous quip that "you can get a Model T in any colour you like, as long as it is black."

In a similar manner, the lightbulb created a viable reason to wire homes for electricity, thereby democratizing both the lightbulb and its complementary energy source of electricity. Mass distribution led to efficiency in installation, which led to faster and broader reach of transmission and distribution wires as well as to the building of new power plants and energy sources (from coal to natural gas to hydro-power to nuclear energy). Electricity having been extended to all homes, it was convenient to also wire homes for the telephone, which soon became the democratized ubiquitous means of communicating. The telephone provided unprecedented means to instantly communicate with friends and family – communication that would normally have taken days through the postal service.

An interesting sidebar to the transmission and distribution of electricity is that, while started by Thomas Edison, there was another prominent American industrialist, George Westinghouse, who proposed alternating current electricity, in opposition to Edison's direct current platform. The two battled for dominance in what is now known as the "war of the currents," which included a bizarre legal battle involving the question of which current should be used to engage the electric chair as a means of capital punishment.[6]

The twentieth century can thus be aggregated into three general periods driven by these world-changing inventions from the nineteenth century. The innovation and democratization of the lightbulb and the telephone were tightly coupled through home-to-home distribution of electricity and telephone cable networks that, by the mid-twentieth century, spanned virtually all developed nations. The lightbulb afforded more economic and consumer "leverage," in that electric wiring in homes generated complementary opportunities for further innovation and democratization of electric-powered or electric/gas-powered furnaces (so homes could be both bright and warm), along with myriad appliances, from hair dryers to refrigerators to televisions (see Figure 1.2).

The internal combustion engine is somewhat in a class all its own. The engine led to innovative applications such as airplanes, automobiles, motorcycles, heavy equipment, tractors, and lawn mowers. Furthermore, the democratization of the automobile by Henry Ford opened up unprecedented complementary opportunities for road and bridge construction, oil exploration, refining, and gasoline distribution centers; it also brought about a massive boom in the production of automobile components (from car bodies to engines to tires to upholstery, etc.). The internal combustion engine, and more specifically the automobile, largely drove economic development in the twentieth century.

The demarcation is not clear, but somewhere later in the twentieth century, or in the first part of the twenty-first, we began moving into a commoditization stage where prices stabilized and even started to retract, certainly for the lightbulb and the telephone, and also for many of the more rudimentary related innovations. The personal vehicle has some staying power as a symbol of status and identity, but the influence of the lightbulb, telephone, and internal combustion engine on our economy is waning.

Economists speak of economic cycles that last somewhere between seven and ten years. GPT inventions – the ones that change the trajectory of our economic development – represent paradigm shifts that unfold over a much longer time than that. The gestation period

Figure 1.2 Spin-off innovations from the invention of the lightbulb

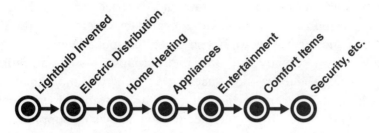

from invention through to democratization can take years or decades; democratization then establishes a new paradigm that can span decades or centuries. As a stark example, consider that we are still actively exploiting new uses for the wheel (recall Taleb's earlier comment about wheeled luggage). At the same time, we need to acknowledge that not all GPTs or life-changing inventions will affect us forever. Gutenburg's mechanical printing press has largely been replaced with digital technologies, and steam engines gave way to internal combustion, which may give way to electrical or even hydrogen-powered vehicles.

In scientific terms, which is how Thomas Kuhn described paradigm shifts,[7] we can look at the second half of the twentieth century as a largely exploitative phase of product development and management. Our means of transport are largely the same today as a lifetime ago. Almost all people alive today, including those born eighty to ninety years ago, grew up with planes flying in the sky, drove/rode in private cars, had electricity, light switches, and central heating in their homes, watched television, used the electric toaster, used an electric oven, and had a refrigerator. In North America, we exist in the same paradigm of daily life and business needs as was faced by people eighty to ninety years ago. The distinctions have been reduced to mere refinements of efficiency or comfort and safety that have developed through ongoing exploitation of the great inventions of the nineteenth century.

Many baby boomers recall their grandparents telling stories about a much different time, when few had electricity in their homes, transportation was by horse-drawn carriage, communication was by post and written word, not so much the spoken word, and going to Europe was by ship only and perhaps a once-in-a-lifetime experience. The expression "packing a lunch" was more than just an expression; it was a tactic of survival if you wanted to visit your family and friends. If you traveled to town to pick up supplies, you took a lunch, and maybe a tent and sleeping bag with you. When I was a young person in the 1960s to 1980s, there was still a mix of diverse generations who had grown up in North America. This is no longer the case. Almost every North American–born person alive today has grown up in a similar environment. We all ride in vehicles and have telephone, electricity, heat, light, and so on in our homes.

Very quickly, by the mid-twentieth century, democratization had largely taken hold, and Western society had shifted into the exploitation stage, where we spent most of the last half of the century. Think about this carefully – by the mid-twentieth century, probably in the 1960s, wired home electricity had created a plug-in society, the proliferation of the private automobile and commercial airplanes had shrunk almost all travel, and telephone connections had brought about instant communication. These shifts, which would have been truly unbelievable, mind-boggling, just decades earlier, were now taken for granted, and this has not changed over the past fifty-five to sixty years. Now think of all the economic and industrial development that has grown from the innovation and democratization stages – how do we re-create that level of growth and prosperity?

Management Education and Exploitation

Caught in this powerful wave of innovation–democratization–exploitation–commoditization is the birth of the field of management studies, which began in earnest in the mid-twentieth century. Management education has been heavily preoccupied with perfecting the administration and efficient organization of the factors of production. Circumstances are such that management theorists have focused almost exclusively on serving the insatiable needs of exploitation. What do they really know about innovation, or even democratization?

The rapid growth of management science in the twentieth century was driven by a need to help firms exploit products and services through economies of scale and scope (i.e., modern-day strategic planning and management), or through sophisticated marketing research and analysis to locate those customers who were most susceptible or largely unable to resist the firm's product offerings. Since the "roaring twenties," business organizations in the developed world have been largely preoccupied with seeking ways to exploit consumers through marketing strategies and scale or scope production efficiencies, and (later) through financial credit means that have turned out to be a wobbly stack of cards that still haunts many of us, especially since the financial crisis of 2008.

As the twentieth century progressed, consumers wanted more, and while there was nothing "new" that could rock their world the way the lightbulb and the internal combustion engine had once done, populations in developed countries bought into the marketed vision, product add-ons, and efficiencies to demand more. And they were willing to pay more, even if that meant resorting to all-too-easy to access lines of credit. Let's be honest – groundbreaking innovation stagnated long ago, decades ago, in favor of incrementalism, administration, and pursuit of more of the same, just a bit better. Efficiency and product customization and specialization have become the mantra of management science in the developed world. This is why Porter's generic strategies of cost leadership and differentiation have struck such a chord with business managers and academics alike.

Most of today's corporate leaders were educated in the 1960s or 1970s. We all grew up in a time of economic and social expansion, driven largely by consumerism grounded in the democratization of the lightbulb (and electricity to all homes), the telephone (and its extension to real-time communication, including television), and the internal combustion engine (and its extension into enhanced personal travel by road and by air). This is the context in which we learned how to respond and adapt to changes in our environment. This is the context in which social scientists and management and psychology scholars studied decision-making and developed "value" around specific forms of analysis and decision-making. Competitive advantage entailed taking a product and making it faster and leaner, with more features and at a lower cost. We sought to eliminate, to reduce, or to upgrade but not to create. In this sense, the shift from democratization to exploitation, and the pursuit of exploitation, are grounded in a reductionist viewpoint, as compared to the expansionist viewpoint required to move from invention to innovation, and from innovation to democratization. Quite possibly, corporate leaders have been taught to be the greatest exploiters of all time, but they have not been schooled in the craft of entrepreneurial thinking, which relies on open-minded and expansionist processes that fuel invention, innovation, and democratization.

Long periods of exploitation strongly support business firm evolution targeted at achieving more efficiency. Even the fascinating work of Clayton Christensen, with his concept of disruptive innovations (see chapter 3), reflects the shift from exploitation to commoditization. The idea of disruption is a profound one in terms of understanding the influence that seemingly "inferior" technologies, products, and processes can have on business, but when we look at that idea from the general economic perspective, we find that the outcome is a faster leap toward greater efficiency and minimization ("faster, smaller, cheaper"). Indeed, disruptive technologies, innovations, and business models represent potential quantum leaps in efficiency, but *not* changes in what we fundamentally do (such as shifting from the horse to the automobile). Disruptions are fully about doing more *with* less and *for* less. In essence, we have developed to a stage where even our means of evolutionary mutation and innovation have shifted from creatively offering new opportunities to stripping away discretionary value to expose the most efficient means possible of serving an existing need. Lewis Carroll, in *Alice in Wonderland,* identified this as the Red Queen syndrome – running as fast as you can to stay in the same spot. Even Christensen, in his groundbreaking study on the disk drive industry, modeled competition shifts as moving from (1) capacity, to (2) size, to (3) reliability, and finally to (4) price – in other words, a drive to commoditization.[8]

Is society caught neck-deep in a race to the bottom? By stripping what we can out of our offerings, are we also eliminating systems of redundancy and resiliency so that we are no longer able to withstand shocks and black swan events? Leaving ourselves without tools to address unforeseen shocks is shortsighted if not irresponsible. This is where Taleb places the emphasis in his research and writings. Only through effective systems planning, including the purposeful stockpiling and oversupply of resources, the introduction of redundancies, the consideration and testing of optionality, and other processes, can systems actually become "antifragile" in terms of what lies ahead. Some organizations practice some of these principles – for instance, Apple typically has access to $30 billion or more in cash or cash equivalents, just in case. But they are very much the exception.

Efficiency and the pursuit of faster, leaner, lower-cost products can also be accomplished through scale. If a firm makes only a 1 percent margin on its product, that still amounts to a sizable figure at high enough volumes. The Walmarts and now the Amazons and Alibabas of the new global economy thrive on large-volume, low-margin business models. At the time of writing this, the market capitalization of Apple is nearly $700 billion. To understand the order of magnitude, $700 billion is approximately the cut line for GDP of the largest twenty countries in the world. It seems inevitable that a corporation will one day be considered for a seat at the G20, perhaps even the G7 table.

Capacity to Innovate?

How do we rationalize the gap between the common view that change is rapid, and the perspective that we are only refining an old way of living? Today's society is living the life of a frog in a pot being heated to boil. A frog will instantly jump out of a pot of boiling or even hot water, yet if placed in room temperature water, it will stay there (even until death) while the water is heated to a dangerous level. We are influenced by our immediate surroundings and by the relevance of change within our insulated perspectives. But when we step aside (stand next to the water, as it were) and consider the profound changes that took place in the seventy years described in the opening quote from Mark Huberty, we see that we have made what Huberty calls "paltry progress" since around 1955. From within the pot, we see what we consider to be rapid change through ever-increasing efficiencies. We are living with the illusion of change.

At this point I am referring to economic or utility change. I don't want to minimize the significant level of social change and the tremendous strides that societies have made toward tolerance and human rights. Some of the prejudices in social systems at the turn of the twentieth century were abhorrent, and it is right that we applaud and celebrate the growth in understanding and respecting our differences, and building social systems that honor human rights, dignity, and fairness for all.

But with regard to our economic systems, we need to be better positioned, as both economic and social beings, if we hope to adapt to a tsunami of GPT innovation and democratization that may be right around the corner. Is the computer the current or next GPT? Is the Internet a first wave of democratization? Maybe, but we have yet to fully experience or appreciate a series of spin-off innovations. Indeed, history may be ready to repeat itself as the Internet, biotechnology (extended to genomic engineering and gene therapy), and nanotechnology (extended to nanomaterials and nanomedicine) could bring about a new paradigmatic level shift. Could the modern corporation of today face the same fate as the buggy whip manufacturer of the early 1900s?

To date, computing technology has been focused largely on faster and cheaper communications, or aggregating and compiling data;

yet the future lies in *dis*aggregating and in complex idiosyncratic applications. It is conceivable that pundits will one day find it shocking that we focused the first era of computing on improving communications. Machine learning, artificial intelligence, smart systems, automated driverless cars, drones, cloud computing, big data, and so on may represent a phase of GPT innovation that promises to rock our world and the way we do everything. And what about genomics, nanotechnology, 3D printing, and biotechnologies? Real change could be near. Are we ready? Are our corporations ready to innovate, or are they stuck in the world of efficiency pursuits?

If we are in fact sitting on the next "change the world" invention, firms will only benefit by adopting a shift from rational reductionism to entrepreneurial expansionism. That shift is what the rest of this book will be about. The time for a new wave of GPT-inspired innovation and democratization, realized through new means of connection, analysis, learning, decision-making, manufacturing, enhancement, and action, may indeed be just around the corner. The successful companies of the future will, I believe, be those that are most ready, most agile. They will be the ones that adopt a culture that embraces entrepreneurial thinking.

How are we going to fare if we are ever faced with the next big thing? It seems that no one alive today truly understands what it means to manage and lead organizations during a period dominated by GPT invention, innovation, or even democratization. We did see a false flash of innovation with the dot.com craze of the late 1990s. By and large, one would have to mark the management of that innovation period with a failing grade. The response of investors and bankers to that era can best be described as immature – they scrambled to get a piece of every new idea, driven by urgency, greed, and the fear of missing out. They were *not* driven by or even aware of what could be accomplished through the power of the Internet (with possibly a few exceptions, such as Jeff Bezos). This is so very different from what we might imagine were the actions of Henry Ford, Alexander Graham Bell, Thomas Edison, George Westinghouse, and their peers in their time of opportunity.

For most of the business community, the dot.com fiasco was followed by a housing boom and credit crises, fueled by falsely perceived innovations in financing, and ramped to unsustainable levels through greed, hype, and overbureaucratized carelessness and brutal dishonesty. And it continues with the Euro-crisis, the US government debt crisis, the Greek debt crisis, and so on.

Possibly our world does not yet function at a high enough level of consciousness to accommodate opportunities without the nuisance of greed-driven interlopers. Another weakness is that in our nervous anticipation, we truly long for innovative solutions, and because of that we are too eager to place our faith in false hopes. How we, as a collective of business and policy leaders, have dealt with economic challenges over the past fifteen to twenty years, as we enter the era of commoditization, can only further convince us that we are ill-equipped/to launch a new era of GPT invention–innovation–democratization.

It is easy to point the finger at business schools for these shortcomings, and no doubt some of the blame does rest with us. As business school leaders, we need to look beyond the experiences we have to draw from in today's world. Today's management education curriculum is driven almost exclusively by the study and investigation of what worked in an era of exploitation, not innovation. We can read about the heady days of the past, and even the projections of a future full of abundance,[9] but our current models are focused on excessive competition, razor-thin margins, and exploitation of marginal advantages. During the dot.com craze, which was the result of early technological advances with the Internet, the world yearned for innovation and democratization, but as a society, we stumbled. The question is, are we any better prepared today for the next dot.com era? The evidence is not convincing.

Others have noticed the gap between our experience and our knowledge and tried to fill it. Most notably, management guru Peter Drucker wrote a book titled *Innovation and Entrepreneurship* (1985). Drucker was proud of the role that sophisticated management theory and practice had played in moving industry forward through the twentieth century, but he also had a very healthy concern for the lack of attention given to innovation and entrepreneurship. Drucker serves as a model for dualistic thinking when it comes to balancing rigid strategic management with agile entrepreneurship.

Austrian economist Joseph Schumpeter described in sublime detail the distinction between management in periods of rapid growth driven by entrepreneurial expansion and more stable economic cycles in *The Theory of Economic Development* (1911).[10] He adopted the term "creative destruction" to describe the impact of inventions moving through the phases of innovation and democratization. Consider the internal combustion engine, an invention that spawned the innovation of the automobile. As the automobile was democratized and became the common means of personal travel, the creative energy that facilitated the development of the automobile – that made it faster, larger, smaller, safer, more affordable, and so on – eventually destroyed (i.e., creative destruction) every advantage previously held by the horse and buggy. The new means of travel, created through innovation and democratization, destroyed the commercial viability of the old, previously reliable means of travel by horse and buggy. We need to learn from Schumpeter and his insights about long cycles.

This chapter has broadly described where we are. From this point on, the book will focus on organizational action – that is, on action driven by business leaders and managers. This begins with a more comprehensive understanding of strategy and entrepreneurship as processes and perspectives that have largely been segregated but will henceforth (I hope) be integrated to form an effective path forward.

Chapter Summary

In this introduction I have challenged the common view that the world is changing rapidly, possibly at the most rapid pace in history. To analyze this idea, I have presented a framework grounded in the evolution of general purpose technologies and the resulting impact on economic and social structures. The framework and observations are summarized below:

1 General purpose technologies (GPTs) lead to paradigm shifts
   that can be described in five phases:
   (a) *GPT-related inventions.* Complementary and spin-off inventions
       that advance the influence of the GPT.
   (b) *Innovation.* Commercialization of GPT-related inventions.
   (c) *Democratization.* Advancing innovations to be accessible
       to and affordable for the wider population.
   (d) *Exploitation.* Efficiency development and product/service
       enhancements to democratized goods to enhance convenience,
       comfort, and other higher-order desires.
   (e) *Commoditization.* Little differentiation and competition by
       price; driven by volume, standardization, and efficiency.
2 The twentieth century can largely be described as a period
   of rapid innovation and democratization of three GPTs – the
   lightbulb/electricity, the telephone, and the internal combustion
   engine – followed by a long and extensive period of exploitation
   of these and related GPT innovations.
3 Management science was created, established, democratized,
   and exploited over the period of extended exploitation of the
   lightbulb, the telephone, and the internal combustion engine
   GPTs. Hence, management science is essentially a study of
   exploitation over exploration; this has the potential to leave
   students and scholars short on the skills necessary to respond
   if a new era of GPT innovation and democratization begins.
4 Entrepreneurial thinking provides insight into management
   science adaptation to address the needs of a possible era of GPT
   innovation and democratization.

2 A Delicate Balance: Strategy, Entrepreneurship, and Longevity

The only sustainable competitive advantage is an organization's ability to learn faster than the competition.

Peter M. Senge, *The Fifth Discipline*

Is the pursuit of long-term sustainable competitive advantage an effective strategy for the twenty-first century corporation? That is certainly a common belief, and a fundamental reason why the captains of industry rely on strategy. They seek a nebulous but oh so tantalizing model of reliable, automated, effortless growth termed "sustained competitive advantage."

Sustained competitive advantage refers to the ability to consistently beat out competitors by repeatedly applying a unique skill, capability, or resource that is exclusive to one firm. Imagine – it is like winning the lottery every day by simply doing what you did yesterday. With sustained competitive advantage, your firm is clearly superior to its competitors, and because that advantage is sustainable, the superiority – including superior profits – is expected to last for years, maybe even decades. Sigh.

But sustained competitive advantage is little more than a theory. A compelling theory to be sure, but a theory more than an observation. Imagine a world where as CEO you discover the one perfect action that guarantees long-term, reliable, sustained advantage over all competitors. It is the corporate version of the Staples "easy button." The real-life exemplar of Bradley Cooper's character Eddie Morra in the 2011 movie *Limitless*. CEOs are seduced by dreamy visions of their feet kicked up on the desk, watching the profits flow in, while they read cover articles about themselves in *Fortune*, *Business Week*, *Forbes*, and *CEO* magazine. The psyche of a CEO can be consumed with the possibilities – "If only I could find that one magic bullet that leads to sustained competitive advantage."

For the past half-century, scholars and consultants have searched for that magic bullet. I am sorry to be the bearer of bad news, but the dream is just that – a dream.

Still, the idea is enticing, driven as it is by the dominant theory for sustained competitive advantage, which is strategic positioning. Originally championed by Harvard guru Michael Porter, strategic positioning correctly posits that firms cannot be all things to all customers. However, Porter oversimplifies the strategic response to a complex environment by declaring that to avoid failure, a firm must choose to excel at being either a cost leader or a differentiator (never both). This is referred to as the positioning of generic strategies. Empirical studies have failed to support the power of generic strategies, and Michael Raynor has recently argued that most firms in fact avoid the polarization of cost leadership or differentiation, and instead choose mediocrity in the middle.[1]

I have to confess that, as a strategy professor, I continue to find it valuable to teach generic strategies; after all, there is an intuitive sense-making logic behind the idea of being consistent and dependable in what your firm offers. This lets your customers know what to expect from your firm, which builds trust and customer loyalty. This is one reason why Porter is still so influential, even without the empirical support, almost forty years after his ideas were published.[2] However, let's keep it real – strict adherence to cost- or differentiation-based positioning presumes a clean split in customers between those who want the lowest price and those who want the premium product or service. While the positioning school offers a useful categorization for rudimentary education, the truth is that the marketplace is far more complex and dynamic, so it is makes little sense for firms to seek a competitive advantage through positioning. To find the nirvana of long-term prosperity, corporations need more tools, and they need to be more dynamic.

Over the years, several books have enticed corporate leaders to adopt specific frameworks or models in their pursuit of sustained competitive advantage. To be fair, many of the authors espoused a more complex application but were nonetheless typecast as promoters of a "one-best" positioning for sustained competitive advantage. As mentioned, Porter's *Competitive Strategy* (1980) outlined the intuitive logic of generic cost-leader or differentiator strategies; Tom Peters and Bob Waterman's blockbuster *In Search of Excellence* (1982) focused on the importance of "sticking to the knitting" as a path to sustained advantage; and Jim Collins's best-seller *From Good to Great* (2001) emphasized a hedgehog strategy. In these books the authors also identified innovation (Porter), entrepreneurship (Peters and Waterman), and confronting the facts (Collins), but the idea that dominated their formulas was pursuit of that perfect strategic position that causes profits to flow steadily as a result of sustained competitive advantage. Even the more recent blockbuster by W. Chan Kim and Renee Mauborgne, *Blue Ocean Strategy* (2005), promotes finding sustainable competitive advantage by discovering a unique position that others have not yet discovered.

Dorothy Leonard-Barton offered a counterview of core competencies in *Wellsprings of Knowledge: Building and Sustaining Sources of Innovation* (1995). She argued that core capabilities have a dark side, in that they inhibit innovation and create resistance to change. Her term for this is "core rigidities." Leaders and managers must be on guard to ensure that core capabilities do not cross the line and limit the ability of firms to be entrepreneurial, but this can be an overwhelming responsibility.

A multitude of books have described and theorized about the benefits of securing the one perfect position, the "sweet spot" that will provide the firm with sustained competitive advantage and, it follows, long-term superior profits. It is useful to study successful firms; that said, the hope to secure a reliable source of sustained competitive advantage by selecting and maintaining a strategic position is largely a false one. More common than sustained advantage is *temporary* competitive advantage, which is entirely plausible and often an outcome of effective strategic positioning. To ground our discussion, I want to share a quick overview of the scholarly work on the topic of strategy, competitive advantage, and sustained competitive advantage.

Strategic Planning and Strategic Management – An Overview

Strategic planning was the first paradigm used to describe the need for large and complex organizations to establish focus and alignment within their workforces. It is quite startling to read in Alfred Chandler's 1962 classic *Strategy and Structure: Chapters in the History of the American Industrial Enterprise* that large firms in the 1920s had more than 100,000 employees, no computer systems, limited communication networks, and complex international operations. In the context of massive scale and low technology, it is understandable that strategic planning soon became critical and often involved extensive analytics and projections of where the world would be at planning time frames of one, three, five, and often ten years. Strategic planning in large corporations involved significant departments with plenty of resources. The central focus on strategy created powerful respect for the C-suite.

Over the years, systems and processes have developed that provide better information and metrics, and strategic planning has given way to strategic management, a less rigid, more adaptable means of applying strategic logic while recognizing that conditions change and that in changing times a "plan" can sometimes be too restrictive. More recently, two forces – (1) dynamic environments, and (2) individual representation – have collided to make it clear that strategic planning is woefully inadequate as a driver of firm success and that strategic management on its own does not provide the tools necessary for long-term success in today's business environment. Let me explain.

First, dynamic environments point us toward the observation that competitive forces are continuously changing. Technological advances, economic conditions, and ongoing shifts in consumer choice cause change at a business level. A proxy term for dynamism is "disruptions," which are occurring in industries at a pace that has caused McKinsey & Company to identify one form of disruption, disruptive technologies, as a primary topic of study. This rapid and impactful change dominates the competitive landscapes in technology-based industries. New firms such as Google, Apple, Facebook, Twitter, and Amazon begin as garage hobby firms and then grow to a size that rivals the GDPs of nations in less time than it takes for a child to start grade school and learn to read (i.e., five to seven years). At the same time, consider the rapid demise or near failure of previously successful firms, such as Nortel, Nokia, and Research In Motion, that were unable to maintain their innovative edge.

Technology is changing quickly, but consider also the myriad other factors that are affecting the business environment at lightning speed: demographic change (including population growth), mobility, trade, economic development in emerging economies, environmental stresses, human rights challenges, ideological strife, terrorism, weapons of mass destruction, and so on. Strategic planning seeks to pre-plan how the world will be in years to come, yet the reality is more akin to the Red Queen effect from *Alice in Wonderland* (running as fast as you can just to stay in the same place).[3] Faced with dynamic environments, firms need to be nimble just to survive. In a dynamic environment, firms must be innovative and entrepreneurial for long-term survival.

Individual representation is a term used to describe the shift from viewing corporations as the unit of analysis, to recognizing the role of individuals (i.e., the CEO and top management team [TMT]). That role is both powerful and complex. Historically, strategy research has treated "the firm" as the body of study, essentially erasing individuals from the equation on the assumption that a strict logic holds no matter who the CEO or TMT might be. More recently, researchers have begun to delve into the role played by individuals. The new assumption is that individual characteristics of the CEO and/or TMT matter – they *really* matter.

Scholars of strategic planning and strategic management theory have lagged in fully appreciating all of the factors that make great firms. They have looked past the individuals in an effort to system-atize the formulation and implementation of the firm's strategy. Noteworthy here is Jim Collins's shocking revelation in what has become the best-selling business book of all time, *Good to Great*. Collins sought to find a replicable model for how firms shift from being just good to being truly great. He fought against, but finally surrendered to, the realization that leadership and decision-making were the foundations of every great organization he studied. He un-intentionally boosted the importance of executive judgment further by insisting that successful leadership is a learned skill, not some elusive secret ingredient handed down from on high.

But Collins really threw down the gauntlet when he exposed as unreliable the notion that a firm can achieve an advantage through structural means alone. When he placed the focus on leadership and on having "the right people on the bus," he was rejecting the plan-ning mantra of relying solely on a replicable and systematic strategy so as to eliminate the human factor.

In its heyday, strategic planning was an all-consuming activity at most large firms, one that included extensive scenario planning exercises, the development of elaborate contingency plans, detailed long-term forecasts, and so on. There is an old story of a well-known CEO who fired the entire corporate planning team when he took over his post because they had established a full-year planning pro-cess that started on the first day of the new year, engulfed manag-ers with developing projections upon projections, and finally ended with the one "strategic" projection set in place on the last day of the year. Ironically, the year-long process resulted in a plan that was in effect a "just-in-time" outcome to start the whole process over again the next day. With all this focus on planning, who had time to actually run the business?

Scholars and corporate executives readily acknowledge that they cannot predict the future, yet strategic planning and strategic management are each grounded in the belief that we can nail down reliable predictions that can be used to establish concrete and rather rigid business plans. It is worth noting that Walter Kiechel III in his book *The Lords of Strategy* discovered that the drivers of strategy theory and consulting were almost exclusively engineers. Why engineers? Well, engineers are trained to understand and manipulate the natural environment (I can speak frankly because I am an engineer). They understand how materials and substances can be created, shaped, molded, combined, and enhanced to produce fully predictable outcomes and responses to environmental conditions.

Engaging engineers was viewed as the most advanced means of perfecting systems, processes, and positions that could provide *the* fit between firm competencies and external opportunities and hence the one perfect strategic position for the firm. This makes sense if one is constructing a bridge, a building, a plant, an offshore drilling rig, or a space shuttle. That is science. But engineering marvels like those have far fewer moving and unpredictable parts than a large organization with employees, customers, suppliers, financiers, and so on. In Taleb's language, we have focused on applying fragile rigid systems to address disorder – and *that* is a recipe for failure.

Strategy, Entrepreneurial Thinking, and Corporate Entrepreneurship

To understand the relationship between strategy, entrepreneurial thinking, and corporate entrepreneurship, I will refer to Figure 2.1, which was first introduced on page 10.

Fundamentally, no matter how old the firm or what its circumstances are, engagement starts with the same question: How can the firm adapt best to current economic, social-cultural, and technological

Figure 2.1 A model of strategic paths (planning versus entrepreneurship)

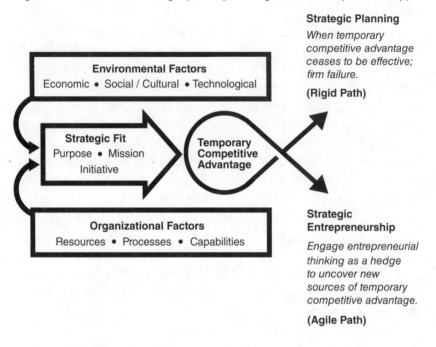

Strategic Planning

When temporary competitive advantage ceases to be effective; firm failure.

(Rigid Path)

Strategic Entrepreneurship

Engage entrepreneurial thinking as a hedge to uncover new sources of temporary competitive advantage.

(Agile Path)

environmental factors with the resources, capabilities, and processes available to it? On day one, the strategic fit among these factors is best described by a set of statements that identify the purpose, mission, and specific initiatives of the firm. Effective identification and implementation of strategic fit will result in competitive advantage, which I have referred to as a *temporary* competitive advantage (for it is not known up front how long the advantage can be effective).

The west half of Figure 2.1 is pretty standard stuff that can be found in virtually any strategy textbook. Typically, firms undertake an analysis of the external environment, possibly using consultants to study market opportunities (which could be market supply [inputs] or customer [output] opportunities). They may approach the internal analysis on an ad hoc basis, or conduct a sophisticated analysis of the value and uniqueness of its resource base and capabilities.

Most firms – even those on the strategic planning (rigid) path – undertake an annual strategic review, studying environmental and organizational factors and seeking to identify the best strategic fit. But they do this in the context of a strategic plan that is already set. Firms adopt rigid planning largely because it helps make clear to the organization's members, customers, and suppliers what the organization's strategic purpose, mission, and initiatives are. But the trade-off in being too rigid with stakeholders is less responsiveness to changing environmental conditions.

Firms that take a rigid approach to strategic planning pursue long-term sustainable competitive advantage as the path to success. But I refuse to buy into the notion of a fully sustainable resource-based competitive advantage – as the market and the competition change, the temporary advantage will decline, and the firm will fail.

The agile approach, on the other hand, represents a strategic entrepreneurship paradigm: the firm develops and encourages entrepreneurial thinking as a hedge against changing environmental factors. Entrepreneurial thinking, here, is a learned skill and replicable process that leads to opportunities for innovation and revitalization. Infusing an organization with entrepreneurial thinking leads to the routinization of processes and managerial capabilities known in the management literature as "dynamic capabilities."

A capacity for dynamism can lead to longer-term advantage by opening up and changing instead of locking up and protecting a specific strategic position. Because the world is constantly changing in terms of markets, players, and technologies, firms that seek longevity must be resilient. They need to embrace and foster entrepreneurial thinking if they hope to find long-term success in today's, and tomorrow's, business environment. But the relationships among strategy, entrepreneurship, and longevity represent a delicate balance.

Within the strategic planning paradigm, entrepreneurial ideas and innovations are typically scrutinized through traditional problem-solving processes, which rely on prioritizing solutions that are familiar to management, and which focus on those solutions that will result in known or highly predictable outcomes. Generally, the process is reductive in nature, beginning with an inventory of alternatives, followed by competitive pruning aimed at eliminating risk and increasing predictability. Management focuses on questions such as these: What do our competitors do? What do similar firms in different markets do? What did we do in the past? These are the paths businesses commonly take when faced with a new or a returning problem or challenge (no distinction is made between these). In the short term, if environmental conditions such as market need, technology, economic conditions, and demographics are stable, this form of reductionist thinking is completely rational and helpful in finding the best solution. But if the intention is to benefit the firm in the long term, and hence in the face of changing environmental conditions, rational decision-making tied to rigid plans is not as reliable and is simply not enough to drive success. Longevity requires an expansive view, not a reductionist one.

Those who do not necessarily buy into the idea of strategic entrepreneurship often ask me, "Well, if entrepreneurship can be strategic, can it also be *non*-strategic?" Yes it can. In a corporate setting, any entrepreneurial activity that does not leverage the firm's skills, resources, capabilities, and processes will be non-strategic. That doesn't mean it won't work, but it does mean there is an abandonment of what makes the firm unique and resourceful. Why would the firm take such an initiative? Why not start instead a new organization?

The most successful companies thrive by establishing decision-making processes that constantly engage new opportunities and that allow the firm to adapt quickly to disruptive technologies and disruptive business models. They allow for play. They allow for tinkering.[4] They learn to balance what has worked in the past with what might work in the future. They strive to exploit their competitive advantage in today's world, while also exploring for new ideas that will provide an edge. I refer to this as "dual processing." Successful companies respond effectively, or even lead change when customer demands, new technologies, or fiscal shifts create a need for something different, new, and unproven.

Indeed, one compelling attraction of the agile strategic entrepreneurship path is that it is integrative, balancing the benefits of consistency with the ability to pursue opportunities through entrepreneurship. Balance of exploitation and exploration is at the heart of longevity.

Abraham Carmeli and Gideon Markman took a truly long view by studying the success of the Republic of Rome between 509 and 338 BC.[5] In explaining the success of that ancient city-state, they discovered that its secret involved a balancing of "capture" strategies (growth, expansion, pursuit of new regions and markets) and "governance" strategies (ability and systems to assimilate, retain, defend, and integrate growth). In applying their theory to modern corporations, they found that capture without governance was highly risky and generally ended in failure, and that governance without capture could in some circumstances result in longevity, but that by combining capture and governance, firms were able to learn organizational resilience and respond to missteps through governance systems that respected ethics and the fair treatment of ideas and people. The balance of capture and governance – a more detailed account of entrepreneurship and strategic management – was found to be the magic formula for developing organizational resilience and longevity.

Entrepreneurship in the twenty-first century is more about enlisting entrepreneurial power and spirit from within the firm. Corporate longevity in the past was enjoyed largely by firms that were able to find the delicate balance between strategy and entrepreneurship. Looking forward, there are trends that suggest that entrepreneurial thinking will soon become far more important, and that firms will improve their longevity by engaging their entrepreneurial prowess at the right strategic times. Following the herd will become far too risky and expensive, and harmful. Leaders will see the benefits of reinvention over extinction.

Logically, the agile path makes sense in fast-changing environmental conditions. But what is fast-changing? The evidence is that all industries face a degree of change such that strategic entrepreneurship will provide a more reliable foundation for longevity. Even more importantly, pursuing the rigid path results in path dependence that is hard to shake. In other words, institutionalizing a strategic plan for the long term can result in rigid adherence to old ways and resistance to new ways. This resistance will be described in more detail in chapter 9.

Chapter Summary

The main messages in this chapter are:

1 Business leaders are seduced by the allure of sustained competitive advantage.
2 Business firm longevity is illusive. Adaptability and entrepreneurial thinking are paths to improve longevity.
3 Conventional strategy research and education has failed to address two important shortcomings – hyperdynamic environments and individual representation.
4 Strategic planning has been presented as the panacea in the search for sustained competitive advantage. But after more than fifty years of trying, it is time to throw in the towel and admit that using a rigid formula to reframe the world to fit the firm's lens is unrealistic at best, insane at worst.
5 Longevity can be achieved not by tossing out strategic management but by adopting a strategic entrepreneurship platform that enlists entrepreneurial thinking and corporate entrepreneurship to hedge changing environmental conditions.

3 The Problem: Firms Fail

A strategy, at its essence, attempts to capture where the firm wants to go and how it plans to get there. When entrepreneurship is introduced to strategy, the possibilities regarding where the firm can go, how fast, and how it gets there are greatly enhanced.

Donald Kuratko and David Audretsch[1]

On the surface, one might ask, what is the problem? Capitalism is alive and prospering. But is it? In fact, the evidence is irrefutable. Firms fail. In fact, almost all firms fail;[2] it is only a matter of time.

Studies suggest that 50 percent of firms fail in the first two to five years, reflecting a survival-of-the-fittest path to establishing dependable routines, expertise, and customers. The US government's Small Business Administration Office of Advocacy notes that "about half of all new establishments survive five years or more and about one-third survive 10 years or more."[3]

Let's consider a simplistic framework that separates start-up ventures (call it Stage 1) from established firms (Stage 2). The conventional wisdom is that start-ups fail so often because they are inherently high-risk, low-resource, and low-stability. But after the first two to five years, as inertia takes hold, the firm reaches a position of lower risk, greater resources, and greater stability. Just ask around – with any new firm, the company founders anxiously anticipate that eureka moment when they have "made it" – that is, reached a plateau of business stability, a point where they can worry less and enjoy more. That is Stage 2 (see Figure 3.1).

Entrepreneurship is essentially the same action in both Stage 1 and Stage 2, with potentially the same outcome. If the marketplace were the only determinant of success (as free market economists would have you believe), then it would be indifferent to whether success was achieved by individual or corporate entrepreneurship. However, there are less rational but nevertheless influential factors that sharply distinguish new venturing from corporate venturing. Consider the expectations of shareholders, the marketplace, employees, and almost all stakeholders with regard to these conditions:

1 Tolerance for management error – in the new venture, errors are expected, whereas in the corporate venture, they are seen as a sign of incompetence.
2 Tolerance for hubris (excessive pride or self-confidence) – arrogance in a new venture entrepreneur is expected and indeed celebrated, whereas it is deeply troubling and almost scandalous in a corporate executive.
3 Tolerance for market mistakes – again, new ventures are expected to misread the marketplace, but that is unacceptable for corporate executives. Look at the problems BlackBerry had with new products, or Coca-Cola executives had when they tried to launch a new Coke.

I could go on. Production scheduling, distribution channels, product presentation, quality control, promotional materials – all of these important components for success are expected to be carried out perfectly by the corporate entrepreneur, whereas the individual entrepreneur is cut far more slack by all stakeholders. It's almost like the new baby – so cute, let's give him or her a chance.

But the biggest distinction between new venturing and corporate venturing relates to how stakeholders respond to a corporate takeover. For a Stage 1 company, a takeover is a sign of success. It is

Figure 3.1 Conventional view of firm evolution

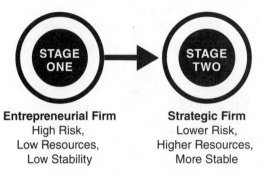

Entrepreneurial Firm
High Risk,
Low Resources,
Low Stability

Strategic Firm
Lower Risk,
Higher Resources,
More Stable

even described positively as an "exit strategy" (i.e., cashing out on the value creation). For corporate entrepreneurs, a takeover is often viewed as a failure. This is a defining distinction between Stage 1 and Stage 2 – in Stage 1, the firm is still wobbly, and the leaders are seen as wise if they can convince a giant to swallow them whole. In Stage 2, the leader is expected to be more effective than all suitors, able to be the takeover leader, not the target, embarrassed and ashamed at the mere thought of being taken over, even for the right economic or operational reasons. One is expected to act like a child, while the other is expected to act like a parent.

In business schools, largely because the highest performance expectations are placed on mature firms, we study Stage 2 firms extensively. We focus a considerable amount of time and energy on identifying strategic management as a necessary if not foundational component, one that enables the firm to "graduate" from pure entrepreneurship (whether individual or corporate) to maturity and stability, able to exploit existing opportunities within a given line of business. Our textbooks provide sophisticated models for assessing the corporate-level mix of business lines, again with the idea of maximizing synergies and combining resources for maximum benefit in the near-term and over sustained periods. Entrepreneurial activity is not entirely absent, but the balance is heavily toward "sticking to the knitting," finding your "hedgehog," establishing a source of "sustained" competitive advantage. While these tools are valuable, the point I make in this chapter is that they are not enough. To ensure long-term sustainability, and to take better advantage of changing environmental conditions in a timely fashion, managers need a broader array of frameworks, models, and idea-generating vehicles.

The Myth of Corporate Stability

To analyze longevity, let's examine the data (from the US Bureau of Labor Statistics; BLS) and see if they support the Stage 1/Stage 2 model in terms of firm survival. Figure 3.2 illustrates the survival rate – or entry and exit rate of business establishments – by year of start. For greater clarity, an establishment represents "the physical location of a certain economic activity, for example, a factory, mine, store, or office."[4] While not every establishment necessarily represents a business corporation, this is valuable information because each "establishment" is an economic activity center with employees and operations, as opposed to a small, one-person business. This is why I find the BLS data to be the best available, and really the most accurate data for assessing the longevity of business enterprises.

These data should also help us assess the validity of the Stage 1/ Stage 2 model in terms of stability and mortality. Are business enterprises at high risk in the first five years of operation? Do they then settle into a more stable existence? As firms develop steady customers, established processes, and reliable suppliers, does the survival curve flatten?

As you can see in Figure 3.2, there is only a gradual flattening of the curve, with no clear indication of a shift in survival rate. Given this evidence, it is hard to support the Stage 1/Stage 2 model, although there is some indication that firms fail, or voluntarily exit, more quickly in the early years, as evidenced by the steepness of the curve in the first five years. I have added a dotted gray line at five-year mark to highlight the estimate from the Small Business Administration (SBA) Office of Advocacy that 50 percent of all firms do not survive beyond the first five years of their existence. In fact,

Figure 3.2 Survival rates of business establishments by year started (%)

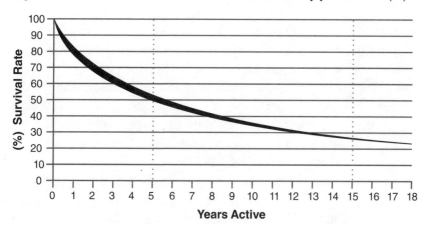

the BLS data indicate a survival rate of less than 50 percent. Note that a further 50 percent reduction – that is, a drop to only 25 percent survival – has occurred another ten years after that (see the second dotted line at fifteen years), reflecting a 75 percent failure rate overall. Think of it this way – three of four business establishments fail to survive beyond the first fifteen years. When one considers a forty-five- to fifty-year work career, it is astounding to think that the place where you work has only a one-in-four chance of being around for one-third of your career. We tend to look at businesses at providing a bastion of stability in our economy and in our lives, but the data simply do not support that notion.

While the steepness of the curve generally flattens out, it still points down. The annual percentage of failure averaged over all the available data shifts from 9.4 percent in year 5, to 6.4 percent in year 10 and 5.8 percent in year 15. The failure rate slows down, ever so gently, but continues to be consistent and significant. It is also telling that these statistical plots, covering eighteen years of data, represent seventeen completely independent sets of data, and show little variance across each independent grouping. There is a sharper decline after 2008, aligning with the finding that failures increase during recession times. None of the curves become fully flat, reflecting the fact that failure continues and can be expected to continue.

These data provide an instructive overview on the state of business in the North American economy. This does not conclusively damn the Stage 1/Stage 2 model, but still, one must wonder – do Stages 1 and 2 really exist? When does Stage 2 kick in? We know that stakeholder expectations for longevity rise as firms mature, but can we say that a firm is really safe, or safer, when it "makes it" to Stage 2? And how sustainable is Stage 2 once the firm reaches that level? We need to consider many other factors to better understand firm failure. Even so, the data provided here are instructive and appear to indicate that firm failure is a consistent phenomenon that is both observable and real.

As expected, Figure 3.2 does confirm that new establishments fail at a faster rate. This finding is supported by research conducted by the Brookings Institution in July 2014. That think tank published a fascinating article by Ian Hathaway and Robert Litan titled "The Other Aging of America: The Increasing Dominance of Older Firms." Their analysis revealed that the share of firms[5] sixteen years or older rose from 23 percent in 1992 to 34 percent in 2011 and that private sector workers are now concentrated in established firms (from 60 percent to 72 percent in firms over sixteen years old). The authors also report interesting evidence of lower mortality rates in the first year of business operations. In summary, they point to a trend toward fewer new entrants, a higher proportion of new entrants failing early, and longer life spans (more than sixteen years) for surviving firms: "It is increasingly advantageous to be an incumbent, particularly an older one, and apparently more difficult to be a new entrant."[6]

Hathaway and Litan express concern about a decline in entrepreneurial activity and a shift to older, less agile firms: "If we want a vibrant, rapidly growing economy in the future, we must find ways to encourage and make room for the startups of the future that will commercialize similarly influential innovations."[7] However, these data were no doubt influenced by the 2008 financial crisis, which introduced significant noise that made bold predictions problematic.

These statistical analyses do, however, provide a context for examining the real world. A huge benefit of being a business school dean is that I am able to connect with some of the greatest business minds available. Every year, we host great business and government leaders. Few are greater than Mac Van Wielingen, chair of ARC Financial and ARC Resources. ARC Financial is Canada's leading energy-focused private equity manager, with over $5 billion invested in 170 portfolio companies over twenty-five years. Betting on unproven horses is ARC's business, and business is good. When I ask Mac why it is good, he describes his firm's rigorous and extensive approach to analysis, one that includes continuous scanning, scrutinizing, monitoring, innovating, and adaptation throughout the life of each investment. As the founder of ARC Financial, he has embraced a pretty straightforward logic:

1 Recognize up front that firms are destined to eventually underperform and fail.
2 Know that too much focus on benchmarking and achieving what competitors achieve will drive a firm faster to where most firms end up – in failure.
3 Remember that only through superior leadership, innovation, and effective implementation can firms survive and prosper.

Those three points are consistent with the downward trend illustrated in Figure 3.2. However, while the data that figure presents are extensive (the full set tracked more than 11 million firms over eighteen years), as well as accurate, the ARC framework is immensely valuable because it adds context to those bare numbers. To achieve longevity, it is critically important to engage effective leadership and management theory and practice.

Before moving to the tools for success, I want to clarify why firms fail, even big firms.

Why Do Firms Fail?

Firms fail at Stage 1 for a multitude of reasons, including lack of an established network of customers, suppliers, systems, processes, employees, and so on. Few stakeholders actually know who the firm's leaders are, what the character or culture of the firm is, or what the firm has to offer. Layer on top of that economic, demographic, psychographic, and technological uncertainties, and it is easy to see why firms are so vulnerable in their first five years.

Let's leap forward and look at the world's largest companies. In a study completed for the Corporate Executive Board, Matthew Olson and Derek van Bever[8] found more than 500 large firms that over the past fifty years have been included on the *Fortune 100* list of the largest US corporations. They tested these firms to learn about the sustainability and stability of Stage 2. They were somewhat startled to find that surprisingly often, even the largest companies flirt with failure. The research also indicated that pending failures were preceded by a peak in activity, which was followed by a death-spiraling fall in sales momentum. The authors called this phenomenon "growth stalls," and argued convincingly that such stalls were harbingers of bad things to come, even for the largest firms. Here is a quick statistical overview of their findings:

- 87 percent of *Fortune 100* companies between 1955 and 2006 recorded growth stalls.
- 54 percent of the 87 percent had slow or negative growth for ten years following the stall.
- 67 percent of the 54 percent went bankrupt or were acquired or privatized.[9]

Olson and van Bever's findings refute the conventional thinking about Stage 2. That is, even the largest firms fail, and more often than not, they dip or drop in prominence. This is supported by the many changes to the membership in the Dow Jones Industrial Average.

The Dow, a bellwether index for the American stock market, has changed its component firms fifty-three times over its 128-year history. General Electric has been on the Dow for the longest period, since 1907, and three firms (Goldman Sachs, Visa, and Nike) were just added in 2013, replacing Alcoa, Bank of America, and Hewlett-Packard. Half the thirty firms in the Dow were added over a sixteen-year period between 1997 and 2013. The Dow represents the most stable and established firms in North America, and still there is significant turnover, further validating the outcomes from Olson and van Bever's study.

The youngest firm in the Dow is Cisco, established in 1984. The oldest is DuPont (producer of consumer products such as Kevlar synthetic fabric, Corian countertops, and Teflon cookware), which started as a manufacturer of gunpowder in 1802. One would expect the younger firms to have not changed industry yet, and that would be the case for specialized firms such as Cisco, Intel, and United Health Group. On the other hand, relatively young firms such as Pfizer (originated in 1949 in the chemicals industry) and Nike (originated in 1964 as a distributor of Japanese running shoes) have morphed into new industries (pharmaceuticals and fashion apparel, respectively).

Of the more aged group in the Dow, many have gone through fundamental change. These firms include American Express (originally an express mail service, c. 1850), General Electric (originally a collection company for Thomas Edison's inventions, c. 1889), 3M (originally a mining company, c. 1902), IBM (originally a tabulating and recording company, c. 1911), J.P. Morgan (originally a chemical manufacturing firm, c. 1923), Walt Disney (originally a maker of animated films, c. 1923), and United Technologies (originally an aircraft manufacturer, c. 1934). Virtually all Dow firms have gone through some industry change/expansion, including young entries such as Microsoft (c. 1975) and Verizon (c. 1983). In most cases there is a strong relationship between the inaugural industry and the firm's current industry(ies), but generally there has been reinforcement of the strategic logic that core focus should change to adapt to environmental change.

Fit (between environmental and organizational factors) is the essence of strategy (see chapter 2), while the ability to adapt to conditions of uncertainty and create new value is the essence of entrepreneurship. At first glance, it seems that a distinguishing characteristic of longevity is the ability to embrace both strategy and entrepreneurship. Still, there is the challenge of knowing when to be strategic and when to be entrepreneurial. Clearly, Stage 2 is starting to look a bit cloudy as a reliable construct.

To better understand the causes of growth stalls, Olson and van Bever expanded their research to closely examine what happened in fifty representative companies. What they found should shock many managers: environmental change may cause firms to change their core industry and focus, but the research suggests it is managers that are to blame for most growth stalls, not the environment. In other words, while it is common to report poor corporate results as a consequence of a poor economy, excessive government regulation, labor market conditions, geopolitics, and so on, in fact these uncontrollable factors were the root cause of a growth stall only 13 percent of the time. In other words, 87 percent of growth stalls were caused mainly by controllable managerial actions – 70 percent by strategic factors, and 17 percent by organizational factors such as talent shortfall, board inaction, organization design, and poor performance metrics.

In today's world of major environmental shifts, such as the 2008 financial crisis, the 2001 dot.com bust, the war on terrorism, and the growth of developing economies, it seems disingenuous to argue that management actions are the cause of firm failures. On the other hand, Nassim Nicholas Taleb, the celebrated and colorful author of *The Black Swan*, argues in a more recent book, *Antifragile: Things That Gain from Disorder*, that managers have the primary responsibility to move beyond discipline and rigor and to build organizations that are adaptable; in fact, they should excel when facing adversity and volatility within the economic, environmental, and social environments in which they operate. Excellent managers take advantage of adversity by expanding market share, shaving costs, and entering new, underprotected markets. For prepared managers, poor economic conditions are often the period of greatest opportunity.

Poring over the years of data in their study, Olson and Van Bever identified three strategic factors as the main causes of growth stalls: (1) premium position captivity, (2) innovation management breakdown, and (3) premature core abandonment. Each of these causes ties directly to the argument presented in this book for more focus on strategic entrepreneurship over strategic planning.

Premium position captivity was the cause of almost one-quarter (23 percent) of growth stalls. Premium position captivity is closely connected with the positioning school theory described in chapter 1. Fooled by the theory-based prospect of sustained competitive advantage through differentiation, managers believe that their firm's product or service will continue to be preferred over newer, less tested, and often more basic upstarts. The examples noted in the growth stalls research include Eastman Kodak (unable to respond effectively to the upstart Japanese film manufacturer, Fuji), Daimler-Benz (unable to respond effectively to the Japanese manufacturers of Lexus and Infiniti, especially in the United States), Caterpillar (facing Japanese manufacturer Komatsu), and Sears (upended by US upstarts Kmart, Walmart, and Target).

The study of premium position captivity is also closely connected to the study of disruptive technologies, innovations, and business models. The term "disruptive" was largely developed and extensively studied by another Harvard guru, Professor Clayton Christensen. Christensen's contribution was monumental in a few distinct ways:

1 His work led to identifying distinct forms of disruption, including disruptive technologies, disruptive innovations (combinations of technologies or processes), and disruptive business models (new ways of combining old tasks).
2 While incumbent firms develop most disruptive technologies, ironically, it is very difficult if not impossible for most

corporations to change their business models to exploit those same, developed-at-home disruptions.

3 Disruptions are generally perceived as inferior in terms of the prevailing market and economic logic of the industry[10] and involve trade-offs that follow a largely predictable consumer-based desire model (functionality is disrupted by added features, which is disrupted by convenience, which is disrupted by size, etc.).

4 Disruptions do not always replace but often expand market opportunity. This is partly due to attracting previous "non-customers" to the new and seemingly inferior disruptive alternative.

Former Intel CEO Andy Grove famously said that "only the paranoid survive."[11] In other words, every firm, every day, faces the risk of a premium position growth stall – of being disrupted by new technologies, innovations, or business models. Patience may be a virtue, but ignoring disruptive change entirely risks a potentially lethal stall.

The second and third most common causes of growth stalls are innovation management breakdown and premature core abandonment. Innovation management breakdown refers mainly to ineffective management of invention or discovery within the firm. As an example, Xerox's Palo Alto Research Center (PARC) was reportedly the birthplace of many of the key features of the personal computer, including the mouse and the GUI (graphical user interface). In the end, Xerox was unable to capitalize effectively on these innovations. Many reasons have been put forward as to why not, but in the end they can all be boiled down to this: management followed an arguably sound practice of focusing on the firm's core strategy, which at that time involved photocopy machines. The photocopier business was booming, which from a strategic planning perspective made it logical for Xerox to abandon its underdeveloped computer products in favor of the proven and successful copy machine. Other examples of innovation management breakdown include situations where firms were quick to invent but slow to innovate, the result being either mismanaged product development or an overinnovated core product that reached beyond consumer desires. Breakdowns are diverse, but all can be collected under the rubric of the firm's failure to incorporate innovation into their growth plans.

Premature core abandonment is just what it says – some managers prematurely direct their firms to shift to new products, services, regions, and so on. Premature core abandonment can be viewed as a form of attention deficit disorder: new opportunities overwhelm the firm's balance between exploitation and exploration. Unfortunately, firms that prematurely abandon their core can miss out on growth opportunities that they were, in fact, among the best positioned to exploit. Consider this stark example from Olson and van Bever's research, describing the actions of Robert Sarnoff, son of General David Sarnoff, who led RCA for more than forty years: "A *Fortune* magazine piece in the late 1960s reported Sarnoff's view that the age of the big breakthroughs in consumer electronics – the age in which the General had built RCA – had passed. 'The physicists have discovered about all they are going to for consumer application in the near future,' says James Hillier, himself a renowned physicist who oversees RCA's labs in Princeton, N.J."[12]

Now, when you consider the post-1960s growth of consumer electronics to include the CD, MP3, MP4, iTunes, the iPod, and so on, this statement sounds shocking, even funny. But that is through the rearview mirror with 20/20 hindsight. When we analyze this quote more carefully, it is clear that research was done, experts were consulted, and the best available information was absorbed, and that all of this led to a strategy to abandon consumer electronics, which were viewed to be at a peak, in favor of other industrial pursuits. In other words, RCA had taken the steps that scholars of strategic management had always advocated – identify the firm's strengths, weaknesses, opportunities, and threats, then develop a strategy that provides the best fit. Unfortunately for RCA, its strategic analysis led it to abandon consumer electronics and instead apply its technological skills to the manufacturing of mainframe computers and consumer products – which did not match their huge prior success in consumer electronics. Arguably, one could say that RCA was in fact being both strategic and entrepreneurial. We can draw some key lessons from this: (1) managers need a clear sense of pending environmental change, (2) interpretation and judgment are always in play, and (3) for heaven's sake, don't bet the farm!

When we stand back and consider the three dominant reasons for growth stalls, and include time as the key dimension – that is, time in the sense of capacity to prepare for the future – we see a distinct connection among the three. Arguably, each of these causes relates to selecting what could be the right strategy, but *at the wrong time*. Premium position captivity is about holding on to a successful position for too long, while premature core abandonment is about moving on too soon. Both reflect situations where firms have been operating successfully in their current product/market space, which is why they are on the *Fortune 100* list to start with; but management decisions cause them to become laggards or premature switchers. Similarly, innovation management breakdown can be boiled down to timing challenges – the right idea, but the wrong time.

At the root of growth stalls – and for that matter, most corporate failures – is the reality that all predictions are couched in some degree of uncertainty. Predictions are sometimes not much better than guesses. Best practice is to undertake thorough research and analysis of the past, but this will only provide a context, not truth about the future. Analysis can help, but it cannot predict. How can firms best prepare for an uncertain future? I argue that the most successful firms are stable and steady, but also nimble and adaptable so that they can adjust quickly to changes in the environment. It is best to build on the firm's current strengths while also holding on to a portfolio of entrepreneurial options.

Chapter Summary

The main messages in this chapter are:

1 Firms, young and old, fail. Careful consideration of both strategy and entrepreneurship is critical to understanding how firms achieve longevity.

2 Stage 1 (start-up) firms are expected to make mistakes, Stage 2 firms, to avoid mistakes. For Stage 1 firms, being acquired is a success; for Stage 2 firms, a failure.

3 In reality, both Stage 1 and Stage 2 firms fail.

4 To address the challenges of premium position captivity (holding on too long), premature core abandonment (jumping too soon), and innovation management, firms need to be nimble and adaptable to ever-changing market, economic, and technological environments. Entrepreneurial thinking can provide a framework for more effective management of these threats.

PART TWO

The Pursuit of Corporate Longevity

4 Longevity: The Capacity to Change

Longevity is the capacity to change, not to stay with what you've got. Too many companies build up an internal commitment to their existing businesses, and there's the problem: it's very, very difficult to "eat your seed corn," go into other activities, or radically change something fundamental about what you've been doing, like pricing structure or distribution system. Rather than changing, they find it easier to just keep doing the same things that brought them success. They codify why they're successful. They write guidebooks. They create teaching manuals. They create whole cultures around sustaining the model. That's great until the model gets threatened by external change; then, all too often, the adjustment is discontinuous. It requires a wrench, often from an outside force. Andy Grove put it well when he said, "only the paranoid survive."

Lou Gerstner[1]
Chairman and CEO of IBM (1993–2002)

In the previous chapter, I introduced the idea of Stage 1 (start-up) and Stage 2 (established) firms. We did not observe a clear demarcation in survival rates between Stage 1 and Stage 2 firms; nevertheless, it is a helpful framework for describing the different attitudes and perspectives of managers and stakeholders.

When a firm achieves Stage 2 status, complacency can set in, along with the allure of the 3C's model of corporate leadership; caviar, cognac and cigars. Okay, there isn't really a 3C model – I just made that up. But what I am referring to is the idea that corporate steward-ship can, under the guise of "we are too big to fail" thinking, become more about the schedule at the country club than monitoring and re-sponding to competitive intensity. Managers of stable firms become complacent. This is what Olson and van Bever found in their study (as reported in the last chapter). Complacency is a cancer that can kill firms.

Let's be fair – hard work should be rewarded, and CEOs should have the opportunity to enjoy life. Many CEOs have worked hard to achieve the 3C lifestyle, albeit replacing the 3C's with more mod-ern pastimes such as fly fishing or yacht racing. But one must be discreet – British Petroleum CEO Tony Hayward eventually had to resign his position, partly because he chose to participate in a yacht race just forty-eight hours after being interrogated by a US congres-sional committee on the Gulf Coast oil spill of June 2011.

Not surprisingly, there are hungry wannabes at every turn want-ing their chance at their version of the 3C model. Corporate leaders must recognize that there will always be high-risk new entrant firms, burdened with the liabilities of newness, but also endowed with an absence of institutional weight, and hence able to adopt new approaches without concern for changing an internal culture or rearranging committed resources. When Netflix entered the home movie rental industry with delivery by mail, they were not bur-dened with the massive real estate investment that ultimately pulled down Blockbuster. When Southwest Air began with a more effi-cient operating model based on using only one model of plane (the Boeing 737), point-to-point flights, and no reservations, their com-petitors faced the prospect of full upheaval of their business model to try to match the new model. There have been many examples of new entries changing the business model, and as Andy Grove said, only the paranoid survive.

But, being paranoid isn't enough – how does the business organi-zation prepare itself for the possible threat of new incumbents? To address this question, I researched some prominent long-surviving firms and found a very interesting and consistent outcome: they all changed their corporate strategy over time to respond to a changing environment.

Table 4.1 lists some well-known companies, what their original line of business was, and what their current dominant business operations entail, recognizing that most are diverse firms with multiple business units. What I found was a wide divergence in terms of the changes in business focus, but absolute unanimity in terms of change itself.

This list suggests that corporate entrepreneurship may be necessary for long-term sustained performance and for longevity as measured by survival. The logic is unmistakable – as technology changes, markets change, and other environmental conditions (economics, regulatory environments, global forces, etc.) change, in order to adapt, the firm must also be able to change. Firms that specialized in buggy whips for horse-drawn carriages failed in a world changed by the automobile.

It is important as well to not lose sight of the magnitude of change. The firms listed in Table 4.1 are among the largest and most institutionalized organizations on earth. Changing from one product offering to another is a monumental undertaking that requires an immense level of commitment and dedication. How do they do it?

What I have noticed in further investigation of some of these firms is that they follow a cyclical model: strategic exploitation, followed by explorative investigation and entrepreneurship, leading back to a new level of strategic exploitation, and so on. I will return to this more dynamic model, and to other interesting stories of corporate scope shift, but it is more important at this stage to lay a clear foundation for our analysis by outlining some critical definitions and guideposts. To this point, I have relied on general definitions of key concepts terms, but as we delve deeper into analyses, we will need to be more specific about those terms.

Entrepreneurship. In common language, the entrepreneur is the person who shows up on the street corner with $5 in her pocket and is the toast of the town in a couple of years (i.e., the classic "rags

Table 4.1 Success requires being able to change your business

Name	Est.	Original business	Evolving business(es)	Commentary
Honda	1946	Motorcycles	Anything self-propelled	Honda views its source of competitive advantage as emanating from engineering prowess regarding mechanical motion.
Hasbro	1923	Textile remnants	Toy company	The textile company started making pencil cases, which introduced them to children, and eventually Mr Potato Head.
IBM	1911	Tabulating & recording	Technology consulting	IBM has faced multiple changes in its core business with tremendous ability to adapt.
Xerox	1906	Photographic paper	Digital imaging, IT consulting	A family business where the son purchased the invention that led to photocopying.
Nucor Steel	1905	Automobile manufacturing	Steel production	Nucor was a highly diverse conglomerate that twice filed for bankruptcy.
3M	1902	Mining company	Scotch tape, duct tape, Post-it notes, cleaning products	The company started mining mineral deposits for grinding-wheel abrasive, shifted to sandpaper, and then adhesives.
General Electric	1892	Lightbulbs	Diverse – turbines, locomotives, CT scanners, chemical sensors, finance	Thomas Edison started the company as a means to bring together all of his electrical inventions, most importantly, the lightbulb.
Avon	1886	Book sales	Perfume	A door-to-door book salesman whose free perfume samples drew more attention than book sales.
Levi Strauss	1873	Dry goods	Jeans	Levi Strauss moved to California to expand his family's dry goods business, and tried selling canvas tents to gold-seekers. A prospector asked him to make pants.

Table 4.1 Success requires being able to change your business (*cont.*)

Name	Est.	Original business	Evolving business(es)	Commentary
Nokia	1865	Pulp mill, rubber, cable	Mobile phones	Microsoft purchased Nokia in 2013, but before that, the company was a model of corporate entrepreneurship.
Tiffany & Co.	1837	Stationary and fancy goods	Jewelry	Unique designs made Tiffany's the first American company to gain international acclaim for jewelry.
DuPont	1802	Gun powder manufacturing	Polymer adhesives, insecticides, fire extinguishers, etc.	A legacy of innovation and entrepreneurial thinking that serves as a model for all.

to riches" story). From an academic perspective, the definition and role of the entrepreneur has changed over the years. In 1921, Frank Knight identified the entrepreneur as the central decision-maker in addressing uncertainty through forecasting market demand. Indeed, much of the economic discussion in the early twentieth century revolved around entrepreneurs who were more what we would today call managers. In his seminal 1937 article "The Nature of the Firm," Nobel Prize–winning economist Ronald Coase described the entrepreneur as "the person or persons who, in a competitive system, take place of the price mechanism in the direction of resources."[2] What this means is that instead of relying on the free market system of independent proprietors competing on price, entrepreneurs think through the combinations of various products and services to combine them into a new value opportunity.

Joseph Schumpeter (1911) initially described entrepreneurs as somewhat rogue individuals who caused creative destruction through their innovative and at times radical approaches to securing additional market share. Later, in 1934, he recognized the important role played by firms in driving entrepreneurial initiatives in a more sophisticated and purposeful process of creative destruction, such as seen in the companies listed in Table 4.1.

In the late twentieth century, academics shifted to viewing entrepreneurship as the study of opportunity identification and firm formation. More recently, scholars, while still wrestling somewhat with the definition, have been leaning more toward recognizing entrepreneurship as "actions designed to create economic value under uncertainty."[3] The importance of this definition is that it does not represent the specific formation of a new organization or company, and it does not differentiate between opportunities that are discovered (i.e., objectively "out there" but yet to be exposed) and those that are created (i.e., a new opportunity generated in the mind of the entrepreneur).

Possibly the top academic in strategy and entrepreneurship is Jay Barney of the University of Utah. Jay co-authored an article titled "Discover and Creation: Alternative Theories of Entrepreneurial Action" with Professor Sharon Alvarez of the University of Denver to capture the impact of opportunity discovery versus creation and to help launch the highly successful *Strategic Entrepreneurship Journal*.[4] As well, Remy Arteaga and Joanne Hyland have recently co-authored an informative book titled *Pivot: How Top Entrepreneurs Adapt and Change Course to Find Ultimate Success*, in which they focus on the strong links between effective management and successful entrepreneurship (individual or corporate).

In this book, entrepreneurship refers to actions that create new economic value and wealth opportunity for the individual, the existing firm, or a new firm, under conditions of uncertainty. I will not be equating entrepreneurship with the creation of a new firm or the risking of one's personal net worth. Entrepreneurship, in this book, will generally be discussed in the context of corporate entrepreneurship (as opposed to individual or social entrepreneurship).

Social entrepreneurship is a new concept driven largely by a younger generation and supported by huge foundations (e.g., the Gates Foundation). It offers alternatives to government social programs and pure philanthropy. It is a means of replacing government or philanthropic social programs with value-creating self-sustaining ventures that support specific social objectives, while also generating value for some sector of society. The field is rather broad as the economic value can be in the form of subsidies on products, wages for disadvantaged sectors, and so on.

Corporate entrepreneurship emanates from within an existing corporation. It may involve establishing a new subsidiary, or it may represent a shift in the core focus of the existing firm. For instance, Avon shifted from door-to-door selling of books to door-to-door selling of perfume to meet market demand. Nucor Steel went through many fundamental shifts during which it created several entrepreneurial subsidiaries. Originally established as the REO Motor Car Company, named after founder Ransom E. Olds (as in the GM "Oldsmobile"), the company started out making luxury cars, then shifted to trucks (the REO Speed Wagon), then lawnmowers; then it changed its name and business to become the Nuclear Corporation of America. But the firm was no more successful in nuclear energy than in motor vehicles, and it moved on to become a diverse conglomerate. The company filed for bankruptcy twice but was able to restart, most recently in the steelmaking industry. It has disrupted that industry by developing mini–steel mills and risen to become the largest steelmaker in the United States.

Corporate entrepreneurship also applies to the public sector, such as government departments and agencies, and to Crown corporations (government subsidiaries). As a general rule, any organization that seeks to create economic value under conditions of uncertainty has the potential to pursue corporate entrepreneurship as a means of generating that value. Corporate entrepreneurship is sometimes referred to as corporate venturing.

The foundation of strategy is **strategic planning**, which originally entailed establishing goals and objectives and setting growth patterns intended to secure firm longevity. Strategic planning is viewed as the most rigid process of strategy making; typically, it includes a printed document containing specific objectives and goals as well as an overriding vision of success. Most firms have abandoned this approach as too restrictive and have adopted either a strategic management or strategic entrepreneurship platform (see below).

Strategic management, at its core, involves creating competitive advantage and wealth.[5] With its origins in "SWOT" analysis (organizational strengths, weaknesses, opportunities, and threats), it provides clarity and direction for management teams. It is often operationalized through a series of statements (vision, mission, distinctive excellence, etc.) and objectives (through a business plan or strategic plan) that knit together financial, capital, and human resource plans, against which results are tested. For the purposes of this book, strategic management reflects the approach corporations take to acquire, organize, and combine resources in the pursuit of sustained competitive advantage.

Strategic management has two distinct levels of analysis and formulation. Strategies associated with what business or businesses the firm should operate in are referred to as "corporate-level," while the study of how the firm will compete effectively within each of its business units is referred to as "business-level" strategy.

Strategic entrepreneurship lies at the intersection of strategic management and corporate entrepreneurship. Firms that practice strategic entrepreneurship are able to simultaneously pursue the dual challenges of competitive advantage (through strategic management) and new opportunities (through corporate entrepreneurship). Strategic entrepreneurship encompasses many academic fields of study, such as exploration–exploitation (Jim March), ambidexterity (Michael Tushman), and opposable minds and integrative thinking (Roger Martin). Of particular note is the current academic debate over the value of strategic entrepreneurship. The concept is intuitively supported by prominent academics in the field and by the research results shared in this chapter; but it is less supported by rigorous empirical research into firm performance. The essence of the problem is measurement – more specifically, the time period over which the firm is expected to realize added value. Previous studies have sought short-term performance impacts, which is counter to the argument that strategic entrepreneurship is only expected to be effective in terms of the firm's long-term adaptability to changing environmental conditions. Yet a longer measurement period would introduce more subjectivity and "noise" to any findings (in other words, there are too many intervening variables that could also cause superior or inferior performance results). So, the question is, over what time period should the firm expect positive results from a strategic entrepreneurship platform? That is a thought-provoking question; resolving it is well beyond the scope of this book.

The most conventional model for engaging in strategic management involves applying *analytical/critical thinking*. *Analytical* thinking involves analyzing an option against pre-set criteria. *Critical* thinking expands that analysis to consider alternative solutions. Hence, critical thinking is more commonly applied in strategic management, generally by following these four steps:

1 Define the problem clearly. This involves differentiating fact from opinion so as to clearly understand the core problem, its underlying causes, and who owns the problem.
2 Generate alternative solutions, which often entails investigating past results to ensure that multiple alternatives are considered.
3 Evaluate and select an alternative. This is done at multiple levels, including against an optimal solution and pre-set goals, taking into consideration uncertainty, risks, required resources, and so on. The preferred alternative is chosen at this stage.
4 Implement and follow-up. Here, care must be taken to effectively implement the chosen alternative and to monitor the effectiveness of the choice.[6]

Systematic and consistent critical thinking is the mainstay of many successful corporations as well as a proven framework for operating in relatively stable environments.

The critical thinking model is well known and well practiced in business, but how do firms engage in both strategic entrepreneurship and corporate entrepreneurship? That continues to be a challenging question. Business and management schools have yet to develop systematic approaches to preparing future managers to think like entrepreneurs. Hence, this book.

There is much more about this topic in the next chapter, so at this stage I will simply identify *entrepreneurial thinking* as a process whereby entrepreneurs and entrepreneurial teams, whether conceiving a start-up venture or a corporate venture, or just searching for non-standard approaches to creating value (economic, social, cultural, environmental) under conditions of uncertainty, think through opportunity discovery and creation in pursuit of entrepreneurship (whether individual or corporate or social).

Entrepreneurial thinking – a new field, to be sure – lies at the heart of strategic entrepreneurship, and studies of it constitute an entirely new field, one that was first presented to the academy in a 2001 special edition of *Strategic Management Journal* and a feature article published in 2001 titled "Integrating Entrepreneurship and Strategic Management Actions to Create Firm Wealth.[7] Strategic entrepreneurship is struggling to find its place in elite academic circles. My view is that it deserves far more recognition as the only possible explanation for the long-term survival of firms.

My own PhD dissertation was a study of strategic decision-making, and my research led me, along with my co-author Frances Bowen, to define a concept called cognitive resilience.[8] That term describes a business decision-maker caught in deep uncertainty: Will a disruptive change turn her world upside down? Will that change fail to take hold? Those who are cognitively resilient are able to simultaneously hold on to the threat *and* the opportunity posed by a pending environmental change. Roger Martin explored a similar idea with his concept of the opposable mind, which is able to keep two divergent options open until the point where a decision is required.[9] The resilient manager is uniquely able, at the drop of a hat, to either adopt and take advantage of a new context, or resist and abandon the new innovation, or even discover a new integrated solution. The ability to exercise patience, apply an open mind to possibilities, keep one's cards close, and wait for the right moment to unveil a new model or direction is at the heart of successfully pulling off true strategic entrepreneurship. This is not to be confused with inability to make a decision or with lack of focus when implementing a plan of action.

Preparing for action and taking action are distinctly different stages in the process, and prejudging the path too early will risk making the wrong choice. Excellent managers and entrepreneurs carefully assess the pace of market, technological, and economic change and maximize benefits by matching changing times with entrepreneurial actions.

Innovation is generally referred to as the effective commercialization of invention. For our context of entrepreneurial thinking and strategic entrepreneurship, I like the more refined definition provided by Arteaga and Hyland, which is that "innovation is the discipline to transform creative ideas into opportunities that could bring value to the market and the company."[10]

There is a close relationship between corporate entrepreneurship and innovation, with the distinction being that corporate entrepreneurship generally leads to the establishment of new business units (a change in corporate-level strategy), whereas innovation most often leads to new internal processes or product features (a change in business-level strategy).

One of the more interesting and impactful forms of innovation is referred to as disruptive innovation. Disruptive innovations are becoming so pervasive that a closer look is important in order to understand the importance of entrepreneurial thinking as a path to longevity.

What Are "Disruptions" and Why Should Managers Care?

The uncertainty that surrounds pending disruptions is palpable, and a daily challenge for many business decision-makers. As a close-to-home example, in my current position as a university dean, I am a member of both our business school management team and the university's senior leadership team. At each level we wonder excessively whether online offerings such as massive online open courses (MOOCs) will replace classroom learning. Scholars have rushed in to try and find the answers to this question, but as of yet, no reliable answer, or even model of comparison, has come forth.

Disruptive innovations are not always devastating to incumbent offerings. For example, when videotaped movies hit the marketplace, theaters worried that their business model was finished, but decades later, taped video has been replaced by DVD, which has been replaced by Netflix and other online streaming services, and still the movie theaters are going strong. On the other hand, in photography, Kodak actually led the development of digital photography technologies but was unable to adapt to the disruptive change caused by the new technology it had developed. So, what are we to make of these, and many other examples, as we consider the future of conventional classroom education in the face of a pending disruption by MOOCs?

In their 2003 book *The Innovator's Solution: Creating and Sustaining Successful Growth*, Clayton Christensen and Michael Raynor identify sixty-seven specific disruptions from our modern times,[11] describing in detail what happened with each and how the incumbent usually failed to adapt to the wicked forces of disruption. Here is the scary part – this phenomenon does not just touch high-tech industries. The examples include book sales (Amazon's disruption of Barnes and Noble), beef processing (using refrigeration to centralize slaughter operations), community colleges (two-plus-two programs upending four-year degree offerings), Dell computer (disrupting retail sales and facilitating customized mass production), regional jets, endoscopic surgery, GE capital (disrupting commercial banks), Mcdonald's, personal computers (disrupted by laptops, disrupted by tablets, disrupted by …), steel mini-mills (disrupted the world's largest steel manufacturers), and Southwest Airlines (disrupted the airline industry). The diversity of this list implies that if you are in business, you are susceptible to disruption.

Christensen's theory of disruption has had a profound impact on academics and practitioners alike. The Thinkers50 list, developed by a blue ribbon panel of advisors, listed Christensen as the "most influential living management thinker in the world"[12] in both 2011 and 2013 (the list is produced biannually). He is referred to as a disruptive thinker because he had the foresight to see a distinction in innovation that occurs when exploitation starts to give way to a new wave of invention, innovation, and democratization – that is, creative destruction. It is hard to see the distinction when you are in the middle of the cornfield, but we may just be in the midst of an unprecedented period of creative destruction, which is another reason why Christensen's work is of such tremendous interest.

Christensen's presentations are even more powerful because he exposes "good management practice" as the reason why solid, established incumbent firms *fail* when faced with disruptive innovations. In doing so, he confronts the error made by those writers, analysts, and (some) scholars who mock corporate leaders who allow upstarts to take over their market (e.g., the way Nucor vanquished US Steel). As Christensen points out, those leaders did what we expected of them – by and large, they followed what they had learned in business school. You see, it makes imminent sense, when under threat, to move up-market and abandon low-margin, broad-based offerings in favor of higher-margin, high-end offerings. This is exactly what Michael Porter refers to as a strategy of differentiation. Any business professor or business leader would support such a move as a way to consolidate resources. But in the new era of disruption, the conventional response does not work. The question is *why not*.

It is worth noting what Nucor specifically did. Essentially, its minimills were poorer quality and only able to produce rebar, which the big steel manufacturers were happy to abandon as a product line. However, Nucor refined its process and was soon able to produce steel beams, then pipelines, then quality sheet metal. Eventually, it wiped out the old industry – one small unintrusive stage at a time. Similarly, Walmart started in small towns and eventually moved into the big cities. The big department stores had been happy to let them have the small towns.

As noted in chapter 3, disruptions have a unique characteristic: the disruptive offering actually *supplants* the most fundamental performance measure, even though both providers and customers of the targeted product or service often institutionalize past performance measures. At the micro-scale of one product or service, this is actually a paradigm shift – the first glimpse of influence from an invention that will lead to further stages of innovation and democratization. Disruptive innovations don't simply carve out a market niche; they represent a fundamental change as part of a new paradigm. This is part of the fundamental cycle of invention–innovation–democratization–exploitation.[13] The path cannot be reversed. It must be allowed to progress to its evolutionary outcome.

Firms survive over the very long term – decades, even centuries – by adapting effectively, by knowing when to be predominantly strategic and when to be predominantly entrepreneurial. They move through recurring cycles of strategic entrepreneurship, with each cycle concluding with a corporate entrepreneurship shift to adapt to changing environmental conditions or new opportunities, followed by an intense focus on strategic management (to get the model working well), and then renewed entrepreneurial efforts to seek out the next corporate entrepreneurial opportunity. These cycles can last decades or a few short years, but eventually the firm's survival will depend on innovation management that correctly anticipates and identifies new opportunities for corporate entrepreneurship.

As Nicolai Foss and Jacob Lyngsie recently wrote: "Strategic Entrepreneurship appears to have dropped strategy's search for conditions of sustainability of (any single) competitive advantage, and instead focused on the entrepreneurial pursuit of a string of temporary advantages, often encapsulated under the label of 'wealth creation.'"[14]

Consider the phenomenal growth of Apple after Steve Jobs's return in the late 1990s. The firm benefited from a series of temporary advantages, starting with the iMac, then iTunes, iPod, MacBook, iPhone, Apple TV, iPad, Apple Watch, and so on. The string of temporary advantages established considerable wealth creation and dominance in the broader field of consumer electronics and music (eventually leading the firm to drop "Computers" from its name).

Figure 4.1 notionally captures the evolutionary strategic cycle of long-surviving firms, wherein relatively short entrepreneurial phases lead to distinct periods of strategic management, which combine to

Figure 4.1 Evolutionary strategic cycle of long-surviving firms

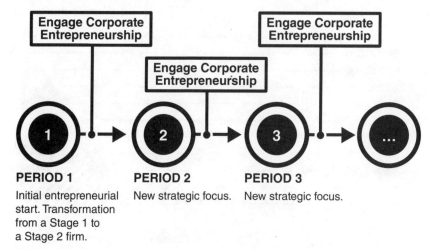

describe an ongoing pattern of strategic entrepreneurship. During the periods when corporate entrepreneurship is engaged, the firm is exploiting its competitive advantage through strategic management, while at the same time exploring new opportunities driven by entrepreneurial thinking.

Figure 4.2 shows the same long-term process in graphical form, assuming financial outcomes from various entrepreneurial initiatives. In this fictitious example, the firm tries a couple of ventures that have reasonable but short-term success, before finally having a big success with the third entrepreneurial initiative. Note that hanging on to the edge of the period 3 box in Figure 4.1 is the prospect of another cycle of corporate entrepreneurship. Longevity requires that firms always be on guard – that they be capable of launching new corporate ventures as they meet the right market and firm criteria.

Strategic Entrepreneurship as a Model for Longevity

Strategic management relies on identifying resources, capabilities, and skills that can be leveraged to take advantage of known opportunities and to compensate for known threats. Long-lasting firms

Figure 4.2 Hypothetical share of income for entrepreneurial initiatives ($000s)

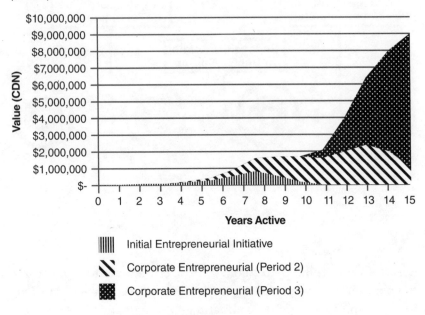

Initial Entrepreneurial Initiative

Corporate Entrepreneurial (Period 2)

Corporate Entrepreneurial (Period 3)

fulfill their strategic management processes, but they also do much more. They engage in strategic entrepreneurship to ensure a reasonable balance between exploiting their competitive advantage and exploring for future entrepreneurial opportunities. Strategic management frameworks are largely static and thus are unable on their own to cope with the dynamic world we live in. In the past, this shortfall has taken years, even decades to expose unprepared firms, but going forward, with the promise of a faster-paced environment, the need for dynamism will be more frequently revealed.

One of my favorite examples of strategic entrepreneurship is the story of Honda and its first move into North America. This was around fifty-five years ago, around 1960. Motorcycles were growing in popularity, fueled largely by Marlon Brando and James Dean movies that celebrated tough young rebels in white T-shirts and leather jackets. These movies generated an almost euphoric aura, probably causing people to reminisce about the brave American victors of war. To be sure, showing up on the American west coast just fifteen years after the war ended was a bold move by a Japanese company, but by the late 1950s, Honda had already established itself as a force to be reckoned with.

Soichiro Honda, the company founder, was an engineer's engineer. Richard Pascale, who studied Honda extensively, said the following about him: "His motivation was not primarily commercial. Rather the company served as a vehicle to give expression to his inventive abilities."[15]

Honda (the person) had a passion for racing and for making the fastest, most efficient, and most powerful use of the "motor engine." To this day, Honda (the firm) views itself primarily as an engineering company focused on exploiting the power and reach of engines. Its entrepreneurial drive has recently spawned diverse industrial applications. As an example of the reach of the firm's engineering prowess, Honda developed the ASIMO robot (Advanced Step in Innovative MObility), which is able to:

- recognize a face and voice simultaneously,
- recognize the voices of multiple people who are talking at the same time,
- predict the direction a person will walk within the next few seconds, helping it avoid a collision,
- change its behavior to accommodate the intention of people with whom it's interacting, and
- run forward and backward, and hop on one or two legs continuously.[16]

Why? Because they can. Well, at least that is how it all started, back in 1986 – yes, 1986. Honda's approach is to focus on creating first and foremost, and then to see where an idea can develop commercially. Its form of entrepreneurship relies on generating revenues and income from ideas cooked up in engineering laboratories. In the case of ASIMO, robotic and AI technologies have spawned many industrial opportunities in mobility, but also new advances in other fields, such as health care (walking assistance), and safety-based industrial applications, such as the survey robot, which is able to complete on-site surveys of nuclear reactor buildings.

To return to our story, back in 1960, Honda wanted to exploit a market that was very frothy for big motorcycles. That market was dominated at the time by stalwart names like BMW, Harley-Davidson, and Triumph. The US market was rich with money and brashness. Honda perceived that there was enough to go around and that hungry consumers would surely be able to absorb, if not welcome, another entrant into an exploding market for "muscle" bikes.

A reconnaissance team of young Japanese managers was sent to sunny California to explore options for the distribution and sale of Honda's large motorcycles. But after arriving, the young managers realized that public transit in California was not what they were used to back home; in fact, getting around to meetings was their first big challenge in America. So they wrote home and requisitioned a couple of Honda Super Cub 50s to use for their local meetings.

The Super Cub 50 is a small, light motorcycle powered by a 50 cubic centimeter (cc) engine (versus the more common 650 to 1,200 cc bikes of the era). The Super Cub 50 was developed largely to compete against the moped, which is a bicycle with a small, clamped-on engine. A moped rider can either pedal or use the small engine to move along at a measured pace. The moped served limited commuter and small-scale delivery markets, largely in Europe. The Super Cub could be lifted and manhandled by one person. The muscle bikes were operationally in a totally different league – impossible to lift through manpower, faster, louder, and generally much more impressive. A muscle bike customer would never consider riding a Super Cub – it would have been embarrassing.

In America in the 1950s and 1960s, mobility was very much a growth industry. The automobile market was exploding even faster than the one for motorcycles. Bicycles were for children, motorcycles were for tough young rebels, and automobiles were for serious-minded adults. What were people to make of this puny 50 cc Super Cub buzzing around the streets of San Francisco? They sounded more like a swarm of bumblebees, not a legitimate form of adult transportation.

But surprisingly, some Americans *were* intrigued by them, notwithstanding the pronouncements of strategists and marketing gurus. They began stopping the Honda managers as they scooted around town and asking if they could order a Super Cub for themselves. They had never seen anything like it, but they could make sense of the affordable price tag, the affordable operating costs, the ease of parking, and the thrill of enjoying the California sunshine with your hair blowing in the wind (no helmets in those days). Selling them on the spot gave way to mail orders, which turned into reliable distributorship contracts with non-motorcycle stores (mostly hardware stores). Ultimately, production of the Honda Super Cub expanded until it became the most produced motor vehicle of all time. More than 60 million Honda Super Cubs have been produced globally – a truly astonishing feat.

Meanwhile, the US market for British-made motorcycles dropped from 49 percent in 1959 to 9 percent in 1973. Predictably, management gurus began falling over themselves to get on board with what they assumed was an obviously superior "Japanese" system. US companies were anxious to learn how they had missed out. The strategy consultants and scholars of the day were wringing their hands and concocting theories about how Honda had forecast and then exploited a market gap and how it had leveraged production to produce at a level that could not be matched by American and European manufacturers. Scholars and consultants heralded "the Honda Effect" as a sign that more sophisticated market research and analysis, production forecasting, and strategic positioning were essential to compete against the disciplined strategic approach of Japanese firms – not just Honda but also Toyota, Sony, and so on. All of this spawned a whole new field of research and consulting whose purpose was to unlock the secrets of Japanese management.

The strategy pundits had a field day as they traveled regularly to Japanese plants in search of the magic formula for achieving Stage 2 sustained corporate success.

But one consultant, Richard Pascale, walked a different road. Like others, he traveled to Japan, but his journey led him to track down the original reconnaissance team instead of using a stopwatch to study the factories and boardrooms. He asked these forgotten managers what they were thinking when they brought the first wave of Super Cubs to the United States. What were their strategies, what was their level of analysis and forecasting? How had they been able to predict the phenomenon that followed?

The tale they told him was different from what the management consultants before him had opined. In fact, the team was driven less by the principles of strategic planning, production planning, and market analysis, and more by the principles of entrepreneurship and entrepreneurial thinking. They simply followed their instincts and addressed the most urgent need in front of them – customer orders. That meant setting aside the original strategy of exploiting a growing and vibrant market (large muscle bikes) in favor of exploring an unanticipated, unpredicted, and entirely risky and entrepreneurial market for Super Cubs. On the fly, ignoring orders from home office, they pursued an entrepreneurial opportunity that had appeared before them unexpectedly. Strategy guru Henry Mintzberg used the Honda example as an illustration of "emergent" strategy as a supplement to "planned" strategy. The Honda team had deviated from the planned strategy for legitimate reasons. In doing so, they had opened the door for further study and development of the field of strategic entrepreneurship.

The Honda team also recognized that strategy implementation is about *action* – about making something happen by completing a transaction, gaining a customer, and moving a product. In Western studies, the tendency is to spend a great deal of time on planning. Planning is important – of course it is – but as the Honda example makes clear, "action" is what counts and where the rubber meets the road (literally in this case).

Interestingly, Pascale noted in his writings that "the Japanese are somewhat distrustful of a single strategy" – which contradicts the findings of others who studied this and other Japanese management successes of the day. What Pascale learned during his interviews was that the team were always mindful of peripheral vision, which in the business management setting is "essential to discerning changes in the customer, the technology or competition, and is key to corporate survival over the long haul."[17]

The idea of peripheral vision and exploring for new opportunities is arguably another way to view entrepreneurial thinking. The next part of this book will examine entrepreneurial thinking as a driver of effective corporate and strategic entrepreneurship. It is worth noting that the Honda story could not have happened without the right organizational culture. In chapter 7 we will discuss how some components of organizational culture can encourage entrepreneurial thinking.

One might ask, what is the dominant culture of today's large firms? There are documents in the public domain that can help us answer that question. Over time, many firms have developed bureaucratic systems and rules that rival those of the largest government organizations. Find a copy of the information circular for any company listed on either the TSE or the NYSE. Then jump ahead to the compensation section and study how management compensation is determined, and what happens if there is a significant event (i.e., a takeover), if a senior officer is terminated, or if a senior officer retires. This will indicate to you the degree of legal complexity that has developed in North American firms – a complexity that consumes our most important corporate leaders and boards of directors. Then read the notes to the financial statements. These documents point to firms that are focused on protecting and maintaining the status quo, not being entrepreneurial and action-focused like the Honda managers in the 1960s.

In the Introduction, I commented that the first part of this book is about understanding why entrepreneurship is becoming a popular topic. Part of the answer is that longevity is tied largely to the firm's ability to adapt, to "read" changing technologies and markets, and to shift to the new rhythm. To again quote a former IBM CEO, Lou Gerstner, "longevity is the capacity to change, not to stay with what you've got." What more can be said? To survive, firms need to be able to scan, read, absorb, analyze, and respond effectively to changing conditions in the environment.

Chapter Summary

The main messages in this chapter are:

1 Long-standing firms go through cycles of change wherein strategic management is required to exploit competitive advantage that can address current opportunities, and corporate entrepreneurship is required to explore new opportunities to address emerging technologies, economic conditions, demographics, regulatory changes, global competition, and so on.
2 Strategic entrepreneurship is a new field of study that attempts to understand the balance of strategic management and corporate entrepreneurship in successful firms.
3 Business schools have long researched and taught strategic management, but there is little understanding of how large firms develop corporate entrepreneurship.
4 Entrepreneurial thinking is a means to bring corporate entrepreneurship into existing firms, thereby facilitating strategic entrepreneurship as a long-term balanced approach to business management.

5 Entrepreneurial Thinking and the Human "Dual Core"

"Paradox" comes from two Greek words: para + doksos, meaning beyond the teaching or beyond the opinion. A paradox emerges when you've started to reconcile seeming contradictions, consciously or unconsciously. Paradox is the ability to live with contradictions without making them mutually exclusive, realizing they can often be both/and instead of either/or.

Richard Rohr[1]

To this point, the new theory of strategic entrepreneurship has been presented to represent a firm's balanced approach to strategic management and corporate entrepreneurship. This combination can also be viewed as a contradiction, or a paradox, given that strategic management is about stability and stick-to-it-ness, while entrepreneurship is more closely linked to risk-taking, change, and novelty. For sixty-plus years, business schools and managers have focused on strategic management as the one and only Stage 2 framework for enhanced corporate performance, while corporate entrepreneurship has been viewed as on the fringe and in direct contradiction to strategic management – you pursue one or the other, with strategic management being by far the dominant model. Hence, I am challenging the establishment, or what Walter Kiechel refers to in *Lords of Strategy* as a firm's ability to be entrepreneurial "on purpose" while maintaining a strategic management perspective. Success requires a delicate balance.

In the previous chapter, I offered the Honda example largely as a fun story that allowed me to contrast entrepreneurial thinking with extensive, and expensive, strategic planning and positioning. From an output perspective, this is a contrast between the planned but illusive stretch goal of sustained competitive advantage, and the adventure of pursuing new opportunities through entrepreneurial actions. The truth is that somewhere deep in the back of his or her mind, every executive dreams about just sitting back and enjoying the sustained operations of an organization that, without intervention, punches out growing sustainable wealth. The *evidence*, though, suggests that a firm can thrive only if it supplements strategic management with entrepreneurial action that allows it to adapt to changes in the environment and seek out new opportunities to prosper as technologies change, customer needs evolve, and competitive forces escalate. In this chapter, I focus on the starting point for entrepreneurial actions – entrepreneurial thinking.

Thinking Models

Daniel Kahneman may not be a familiar name to the readers of this book, but he is a giant in the field of cognitive influences on decision-making under uncertainty. Kahneman and his long-time colleague Amos Tversky developed prospect theory, which was good enough to earn them a Nobel Prize in economics. Why economics? Because they proved that people do not follow rational utility theory when making decisions – they weigh options based on cognitively framed distinctions between losses and gains, and take into account reference points and myriad heuristics when making judgments and choices.

Kahneman's most recent mission was to compile all his knowledge and make it more accessible to the those who hadn't dedicated their lives to understanding all of the terminology, neurology, and psychoanalysis wrapped up in his more sophisticated research projects. In *Thinking Fast and Slow* he explains that thought comes to humans in two forms. System 1 is fast and intuitive. Malcolm Gladwell wrote about this as well in *Blink*. We often respond to a situation quickly, intuitively, possibly even instinctively. It is hard for some to control the impulse to use System 1 at all times, but often reflection, analysis, and more data are important to making the best decision, and this is where System 2 kicks in. Consider the distinction this way: System 1 is akin to reacting, while System 2 is akin to responding. System 1 is based on emotions; System 2 is grounded in rational argument. System 2 is slow and hard, so our brains often override and push us to engage System 1, but in reality, System 2 is generally more reliable and effective. I say *generally* for a specific reason that I will soon reveal. Figure 5.1 provides a schematic overview of Kahneman's fast and slow typologies.

Let's face it: if we could get by solving all of our problems with System 1 thinking, life would be a lot less effort. It is hard work to use a System 2 approach, where research and analysis can lead to counterviews that don't fit with intuitive or "gut" feel. This is the same in our personal lives and in our corporate world. We seek clean and simple answers, but corporations, markets, technologies, and so on are all messy and complex. No one person has the best intuitive answer for all situations, and the magic of big data will not make it easy for us to push a button and get the right answer. With every day, every new idea, every new competitive offering, every new consumer insight, decision-making requires more and more considerations, so we need to work within a framework of System 2 thinking.

Kahneman's brilliant master framework provides the context for studying different thinking models, or different means for engaging System 2. I present this as an overview because I want to make a clear distinction: we are *not* talking about System 1 decisions in this book. Every day, intuitive and routine decisions are taken by every member of every organization. Those decisions will carry on for the most part; however, as a firm adopts an entrepreneurial thinking foundation, some System 1 decisions will shift to System 2. Nevertheless, for the purposes of this analysis, I ask that you keep in mind that we are studying and testing System 2–type decisions, ones for which you would normally seek data and information.

Figure 5.1 Overview of Kahneman's decision-making typologies

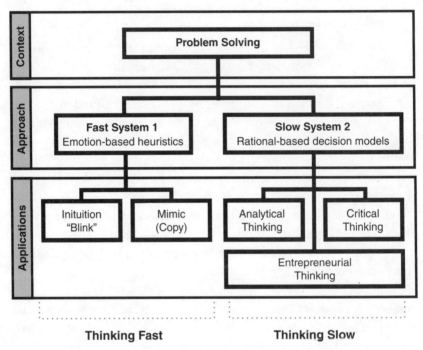

Dual-Core Processing (Human-Style)

The thinking models available through academic research are wide and diverse, but for the purposes of our study, I want to focus on the distinctions between critical thinking and entrepreneurial thinking. Critical thinking is the most common heuristic for business decision-making, and as noted in chapter 4, the model relies on (1) problem identification, (2) exploring available alternatives, and (3) choosing the best alternative based on the data available. This is a shorthand version, which will suffice for now.

Critical thinking is taught because it has a huge advantage over opinion-based decision-making, or System 1. By and large, children grow up in frustration and envy as parents and other adults of authority (teachers, etc.) get what they want, and the reasons why they will hear "no" in response to their actions are not always clear. This is often translated into a world view where adults get what they want because they are in authority. Reasoning becomes translated as opinion. Let me give you an example.

I run a first-year introductory session to prepare students for business school education, and ask them, "Given these three choices of posters, which should the marketing manager choose?" By nature, most students opt for the System 1 answer, which will be based on their favorite colour, most pleasant mix of open space and content, attraction to certain people in the images, and so on. By contrast, critical thinking requires the respondent to step back and first ask questions, such as, What is the problem? Who are we trying to attract? What are we trying to sell? Who are our customers? And so on. Critical thinking is an extremely important skill for business students and business people to learn, but is it enough for employees, supervisors, managers, and leaders of today's or tomorrow's corporations?

Figure 5.2 provides a graphical description of several distinct thinking models. This is by no means intended to include *all* thinking models, but rather a selection that will help contextualize entrepreneurial thinking and the human equivalent of dual-core processing. The horizontal axis represents the overriding pursuit of the one best (or the "correct") answer, versus an acceptance of ambiguity and possibly not really knowing what the right answer is, as depicted in the far right pole. To guarantee certainty, the usual preference is for the kinds of problems that are solved with one simple answer, but that is not always possible. The most challenging unknown is the future, so with more complex and longer-term decisions, one would expect a decision-making model farther to the right side of the graph to be the most effective.

The vertical axis represents the distinction between expansive versus reductive decision-making models. Expansive models keep the decision in a more open state, anticipating that a better alternative could be just around the corner, whereas reductive models are more time-bound and disciplined to select a decision and proceed

Figure 5.2 Structured thinking approaches

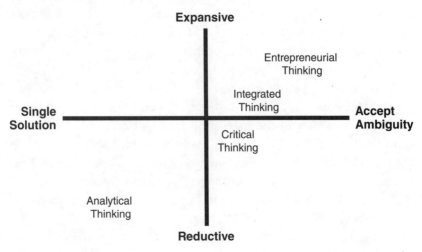

with implementation, usually in accordance with a predetermined schedule. There is no right or wrong to this graph, just a means of understanding what you receive from each model to facilitate a match with specific problems, circumstances, and intended outcomes.

In the northwest sector, I use the term "perfection thinking" to represent the model where the one perfect answer is the only acceptable response, and the model continues to expand until this one best answer is found. Translation – procrastination, delay, deferral, dithering, indecision. This model, which is rarely intended, is too often the default when a decision-maker simply does not know what to do (i.e., it is a common avoidance technique).[2]

One highly successful use of the perfection model, however, was during the Cuban Missile Crisis, when President John F. Kennedy insisted on more discussions within his Cabinet to find a solution that achieved the full consensus of the Cabinet. One could argue that seeking consensus is anything but perfection, but it is all in the way you structure your problem and solution. Kennedy sought simply to find a solution that met with satisfaction for all branches of his Cabinet. Frankly, many of us may be alive today only because of the decision to not back down, but to also not initiate military action. For an amazing insight into team decision-making, I encourage you to explore the many reference materials available on this unimaginably tense drama, including several stellar videos/movies/re-enactments. Or, do yourself a favor and pick up a copy of Graham Allison's book, *Essence of Decision: Explaining the Cuban Missile Crisis*.[3]

Analytical thinking is the term I use to reflect analysis that occurs on a daily basis in organizations. Consider the challenge of addressing the practical problem of shrinking product margins in the face of rising costs (inflation). Analytical thinking presents the data in a specific design, defining the margins in as much detail as is called for; this includes sensitivity analysis on the impact of volume, exchange rates, sales programs, and so on. Analytical thinking focuses on one set of conditions and is useful for providing decision-making support in terms of ratios, trends, relevance, and the like. Analytical thinking helps a manager determine the optimal volume, product features, sales programs, distribution channels, and so on for a specific product.

Analytical thinking is considered reductive in that it takes a limited universe of data and refines and reworks those data to provide more useful information for the decision-maker. This approach has clear benefits, but it is not comprehensive enough to work for all decisions, especially more complex ones.

Critical thinking is in many ways an extension of analytical thinking. Many strategic decisions are based on critical thinking, which uses the analysis available for the product facing margin pressure but incorporates other important alternatives besides. Do we outsource production? Do we retool our plant and offer a different product altogether? If we sold our plant and laid off our sales team, where would we best redeploy our capital? When the ability to compare alternatives is introduced, the limiting factor is less the data available than how the problem is framed. The question could be about the most efficient way to produce the product. Or, what is the most effective means of selling? What are the correct product features? Or, the problem could be framed in a broader context – for instance, what business is our firm in? What business *should* the firm be in? This is overly simplistic, but analytical thinking can at times be an effective and efficient tool for "business-level" strategic decisions ("How do we compete effectively within our chosen business line?"), whereas critical thinking is imperative for "corporate-level" strategic decisions ("What business or businesses should we be in?").

Many of the most effective professionals, managers, and leaders have developed the knowledge and experience to know when to be analytical and when to be critical. For instance, an engineer responsible for oilfield reserve estimates and production rate expectations will use the best available expertise and standards to conduct an effective and accurate analysis. A lawyer writing an opinion letter will do a thorough review of the applicable case law and provide an expert opinion that includes reliable (likely statistically validated) estimates of outcome success. These are examples of using the right thinking process for the right job. There is a time and place to explore new methods of extracting oil or resolving conflicts, and those may call for critical thinking, possibly even entrepreneurial thinking. The purpose of the graphical representation is to make clear that, even within System 2 options, much success lies in the decision-maker's ability to select the right tool for the job.

The northeast quadrant has two thinking models: entrepreneurial and integrated. As noted already, I argue that entrepreneurial thinking is more critical today as a counterbalance to the pendulum having swung too far in support of critical thinking (which is essentially in support of strategic management processes).

Integrated thinking, as described by Roger Martin,[4] reflects one possible model for true strategic entrepreneurship. Integrated thinking represents the rejection of "either/or" in favor of "and" solutions and the ability to hold constant two potential paths (described by Martin as the "opposable mind," and depicted in my research as "cognitive resilience"). In other words, it is the combining of multiple perspectives that brings balance to integrated thinking. Ultimately, effective strategic entrepreneurship requires both critical thinking (for strategic management reflection) and entrepreneurial thinking (for the corporate entrepreneurship perspective) to form integrated thinking (balance and potential synergies between strategic management and corporate entrepreneurship). In a way, this is like the dual-core microprocessor that revolutionized computers by allowing users to attend to multiple rather than either/or computing choices.

As mentioned earlier, Figure 5.2 is not intended to include all models of thinking, and I should mention a few that readers might wonder about. Creative thinking is expansive and accepts ambiguity, so it would be in the top right quadrant, along with design thinking and various derivations of each. There are clear connections among creative thinking, design thinking, integrated thinking, and entrepreneurial thinking, and indeed, Roger Martin has provided some context to relate design thinking and integrated thinking in particular.

This is a business book, so I find it most appropriate to stick with entrepreneurial thinking as there is a clear objective, which is to find entrepreneurial solutions to business situations. Creative and design thinking connects well with some but not all situations. The moderating factor is largely dispositional in terms of individual traits. In other words, when it comes to design thinking, artists instantly "get it," but engineers, not so much. I believe that the audience that would relate to entrepreneurial thinking provides a closer match to business.

The graphical depiction in Figure 5.2 provides an overview, but to more fully explore the distinctions between critical thinking and entrepreneurial thinking, as well as the opportunities for dual-core processing to lead to integrated thinking, I have included Table 5.1.

Foundational to rational reductionism is exploitation through problem solving. Critical thinking is more commonly engaged in addressing a defined problem. By contrast, entrepreneurial thinking – especially the Barney and Alvarez notion of opportunity creation[5] – is focused more on exploration through creating or discovering

Table 5.1 Comparisons of business thinking processes

	Rational reduction (Critical thinking)	Entrepreneurial expansion (Entrepreneurial thinking)
Pursuit	Problem solving	Opportunity seeking
Dominant focus	Exploitation	Exploration
Criterion	One optimal solution	Portfolio of options
Approach	Optimizing (staying within constraints)	Innovating (challenging constraints)
Mindset	Fixed	Growth
Trajectory of ideas	Linear	Iterative
Search	Local	Local and distant
Assumptions about the future	Known probability and distribution of events	Knightian uncertainty, with Predictive outlook
Nature of innovations	Incremental, competence-enhancing	Disruptive, competence-enhancing and destroying
Business planning	Deliberate proactive	Belief foundation – Trial & error
Source of advantage	Market power or unique resources	Schumpeterian innovator's advantage
New venture development	Comprehensive business plan	Lean start-up

new, untapped opportunities available to the firm. In this sense, we have a divergence of thought approach right from the context-setting stage of the thinking process.

Rational reductive thinking is all about staying within the constraints but nevertheless optimizing the challenge presented. This takes clever people, and I certainly would never understate the value of this approach, but it is also important to recognize that it is distinctly different from innovating, which challenges the constraints placed on a specific situation. Hence, the entrepreneurial mindset must be open to all possibilities, as well as growth-oriented as described by Carol Dweck[6] in her extensive body of research on fixed and growth mindsets. Again, there is nothing wrong with a rational reductionist having a fixed mindset, provided that the model is used for the right job. Indeed, when comparing production characteristics, there is a time and place for sticking to the relevant data and not exploring new opportunities. It all depends on the definition of the problem and the job to be done. I return to the topic of growth mindsets in the next chapter, as part of a more detailed discussion on entrepreneurial culture.

The trajectory of ideas is necessarily linear for rational reductive thinking, and includes consideration of what the organization has done in the past and what the industry standards are, then moving on to what is sought (whether more efficiency, or more sales, or more production, etc.). In that sense, the search is generally quite local as well, although it would not be unusual to search for geographically distant ideas. A rational reductive thought process rarely looks far beyond the home industry and the firm's past experience for ideas. This works largely because rational reductive reasoning requires some level of comfort that the future is more or less predictable, based largely on past experience, within a reasonable margin of error.

By contrast, expansionist thinking views the future state of the world as highly uncertain, and hence the approach diverges significantly at this stage to require a more far-reaching exploration of successful approaches adopted in diverse industries, or ideas that have never been tried before. This necessitates an iterative versus linear trajectory, which can be very frustrating and unpredictable for management. Nevertheless, our research indicates that to succeed, management *must* be able to provide a predictive vision of how any innovation will effectively play out in this uncertain world – a challenge to be sure, which is discussed more in the chapter on leadership and implementation.

Rational reductive reasoning can certainly result in innovations, but those innovations are largely incremental and competence-enhancing to support growth along the trajectory already established by the firm. Business planning is serious work, with myriad meetings, discussions, negotiations, and published documents that describe objectives, targets, and clear direction for all members of the organization. Competitive advantage generally comes from being better at executing than the competition and hitting the sweet spots in terms of product offerings, locations, merchandising, and so on, all of which lead to measures such as brand loyalty, market share, and market power as sources of competitive advantage.

Entrepreneurial expansionism requires a search less for steady growth than for big breakthroughs by engaging disruptive innovations and technologies, some of which are competence-enhancing, and some of which are less respective of existing competencies. There is a terrible academic term used when innovations do not build on the competencies already within the firm: "competence destroying." I say terrible because the competencies are not actually destroyed; instead, the term reflects the possibility of retraining, expansion, learning, and making use of alternative competencies. This is poor terminology that is, unfortunately, already well established in the literature.

In the entrepreneurial expansive column, business plans are prepared, but they are not as formalized and are intended more as general guideposts, not as actual plans to be followed step by step. Bankers like the business plans, but the leaders of entrepreneurial organizations are far more focused on their belief in the future and their ability to survive the trial and error process, hopefully coming out of the other end with something new and amazing.

Strategic entrepreneurship is about balancing strategic management and corporate entrepreneurship, but in practical terms, modern corporations are strategic management machines, and an understanding of the distinct differences between critical and entrepreneurial thinking is necessary to move toward a balance.

Chapter Summary

The main messages in this chapter are:

1 To develop a better understanding of reliable entrepreneurial thinking, we need to focus on System 2 thinking (in other words, beyond intuition).

2 Entrepreneurial thinking is both expansive and accepting of ambiguity (as opposed to seeking the one best answer).

3 A comprehensive comparison is provided to allow for clearer distinction between rational reductionist critical thinking and expansionist entrepreneurial thinking. Strategic entrepreneurship requires a balancing of both thinking styles.

6 The Micro-Foundations of Entrepreneurial Motivation

Twenty years from now you will be more disappointed by the things that you didn't do then by the ones you did do. So throw off the bowlines. Sail away from the safe harbor. Catch the trade winds in your sails. Explore. Dream. Discover.

Mark Twain[1]

To better understand the root of an action, such as entrepreneurial action within organizations, scholars typically dig deep in search of the "micro-foundations" of a phenomenon – in this case, the micro-foundations of entrepreneurial choice. Can we gain a better understanding of what goes on in the minds of decision-makers, the cognitive influences that motivate decision-makers to choose exploration? Can we better understand those managers who are able to operate as dual-core processors, simultaneously holding both options (exploration and exploitation) at ready state through cognitive resilience and integrative thinking? These were some of the challenges selected by a research team co-led by Oleksiy Osievskyy and myself. Oleksiy is a former PhD student of mine who is now an Assistant Professor of Entrepreneurship and Innovation at the Centre for Entrepreneurship Education at the D'Amore–McKim Business School at Northeastern University in Boston.

Empirical Research into Micro-Foundations

To control industry influences more effectively, we developed a research plan that benefited from a careful selection of industry settings that are facing well-known, even well publicized technological
or business model change of a magnitude to potentially disrupt and
even eliminate the current dominant means of production and operation. We chose two distinct situations in order to examine diversity in terms of organization size, private versus public ownership
and perspective, institutionalized versus evolving, and so on. First,
we considered the threat to real estate brokers of enhanced online
information sharing; then we studied the concerns of university officials facing online educational options, most notable massive online
open courses (MOOCs).

The first study was an extension of an earlier study of realtors,
once again demonstrating the divergent cognitive sensing of a
threatening yet potentially opportunistic situation. We felt that the
differences between real estate brokerage, which is a fractured industry typified by small, privately held owner-operators in local
settings, and universities, which are large, institutional and mostly
publicly funded giants, would be as stark as we could get. Almost
the only commonality we saw was that both real estate brokers and
university leaders were facing the threat of major disruption in their
operating models, and the need for top decision-makers to formulate perspectives and decision-making intentions. Let me briefly describe each situation.

Historically, the dominant business model for real estate brokers in
North America hinged largely upon control of information by means
of one uniquely valuable resource – monopoly access through the
Multiple Listing Service (MLS). MLS systems contained the most
comprehensive information about the local real estate markets and
were generally operated exclusively for and/or by local realtors' as-
sociations. MLS databases include information such as the period
a certain home is listed for sale, the list price, the sales price, the

home layout, photos, previous owners, renovations, and so on – a potpourri of valuable information that potential buyers desire but would be unable to find elsewhere.

Since real estate clients are not able to access MLS directly, historically buyers have had to find a broker for access, and this need drove the constant stream of clients to engage a real estate broker (i.e., a realtor). Picture this in the days before the Internet, when MLS "books" that included information on listed homes were published weekly. Exclusive access to this database raised a sizable barrier to entry, as well as protection for the role of the real estate broker. Over time, real estate brokers were wise and bundled this exclusive access with a comprehensive service that included contract negotiations and administration, along with various other services. They also had the service regulated to ensure professionalism, which further extended the barriers to entry and protected the industry from disruption.

However, since the early years of the twenty-first century, the industry has been changing through the emergence of a disruptive technology (Internet sites that list properties for sale) that has opened the way for various disruptive business models (discount brokers, mere posting services, services for FSBO–"For Sale by Owner"). This is somewhat in contrast to the rapid disintermediation that has occurred in other brokerage industries such as stock markets (Charles Schwab) and travel (Expedia, Travelocity, etc.). Change had been much slower in the real estate brokerage industry for a variety of reasons, but then in the fall of 2010, the situation in the Canadian real estate brokerage industry changed dramatically. The industry's regulator and the federal Competition Bureau legalized discounted brokerage services (such as listing on local MLS systems for a flat fee), by this means depriving traditional real estate brokers of their protective shield, that is, monopoly access to the MLS tied to a bundling of services.

. Faced with the regulatory change, real estate brokers and firms responded differently; some experimented with new business models, but most remained steadfast in their resistance to new and

presumably less profitable offerings. This was an entirely predictable response from incumbent firms, much as what was witnessed
in the airline industry (with the Southwest Airlines discount model)
and retail sales (with Kmart and Walmart and, more recently, e-
commerce models such as Amazon). Incumbents in all industries
are prone to resist change.

We developed and administered an electronic survey, aimed at brokers (owner-managers of the business) in two Canadian provinces,
and received 241 fully usable responses.

We studied the higher education industry at a critical time, when
a threat from online education was materializing. Universities have
operated in relatively stable environments for centuries and with
largely the same classroom delivery models. But recently, disruptive forces enabled by technological advances are creating turbu-
lence through options such as MOOCs and online degree programs.
There have been alternative models in the past, some of which have
focused on teaching excellence without a direct link to research,
and/or without the added overhead and burden of athletics, study
centers, and libraries. But MOOCs introduced much more serious
concerns, for this model threatened to eliminate the classroom experience entirely and render physical infrastructure as no longer required for or beneficial to education.

At the time we undertook this study, the threat of MOOCs was
gaining momentum; such courses were being viewed as an entirely
plausible substitute for conventional education. In 1998 only 34 percent of US degree-granting institutions were offering online courses; a decade later that number had risen to 66 percent and more than
12 million students were taking such courses.[2] Even more surprising, 1,230 degree and 340 certificate programs were being offered
exclusively online in 1998; by 2007 the number had grown to 7,418
degree and 3,822 certificate programs.[3]

Some observers felt that new approaches to delivering education
threatened to reduce the "coming of age" socializing educational experience to a collection of ad hoc individual pursuits; others felt that
online technologies not only enabled new approaches to delivering

courses but also opened the door to rethinking the entire education paradigm. We connected directly with senior officials at universities in the United States, Canada, Australia, and New Zealand
and received 173 usable responses to our survey. The answers were
collected from informed respondents – senior executives (provost,
vice-president level) of the universities – so we are confident in the
validity of the findings.

Armed with findings from the two studies, each involving a distinct industry setting and a predetermined dominant business model,
we tested a framework grounded in the strategic entrepreneurship
model of exploration–exploitation. The framework is shown in
Table 6.1.

Our framework provides a useful approach to studying many
questions associated with the phenomenon of industry member pro-
pensity to adopt change (or resist it). Not surprisingly, after plugging
several data sets into the framework, we found that most incumbent
firms – over 60 percent – resided in Group 4 (pure exploitation), which
is reflective of decision-making through the pure strategic management model. We also found a healthy proportion of organizations
that positioned themselves within Group 1. We resisted assuming
that Group 1 is a proxy for a specific perspective, for it could, under
certain conditions, represent a strategic response, but it also reflects a
mere absence of strategy. Corporate entrepreneurship, which is most
closely reflected in Group 2, had the smallest proportion of respondents. This finding reflects corporations' general fear of change, sense
of vulnerability to newness, and lack of internal capabilities to enable
effective response to disruptions. The inability of firms to respond as
entrepreneurs to disruptions has fueled an entire new field of study.

A healthy proportion of respondents had adopted an integrated strategic entrepreneurship perspective as reflected in Group 3. Table 6.1
provides specific typologies of response, but the overall summary
findings of our comprehensive research program are as follows:

1. **Opportunity identification is a precondition for entrepreneurial action.** In other words, even if managers feel their livelihood is

Table 6.1 Typology of incumbent firm responses to disruptive innovations[4]

		Exploitative strengthening of the existing business model	
		No	Yes
Explorative adoption of the disruptive business model	Yes	Group 2: Pure exploration: Adoption of the new approach Proxy for corporate entrepreneurship	Group 3: Integration (in one company or spin-off) Proxy for strategic entrepreneurship
	No	Group 1: Defiant resistance: Defend habitual routines	Group 4: Pure exploitation: incremental innovating Proxy for strategic management

threatened by a disruptive alternative, they will reject and fight the disruptive alternative unless they are able to see a clear opportunity, a better path, for themselves. This largely explains the condition we often see where incumbent firms defiantly resist change. As an example, North American airlines refused to adopt the Southwest model even though most eventually went through bankruptcy proceedings as a consequence of their resistance to change. So a lack of opportunity sensing can drive "threat-rigid" responses, even when failure is imminent.

2. **Prior positive risk experience drives entrepreneurial action.** We found that managers who had success in trying higher-risk strategic moves in the past were more likely to explore new opportunities. This is a sensible application of learning theory: what has been done in the past can be done again. In summary, experiment early, fail early, and learn for the future.

3. **The paradigm of "strategic management" dominates management thought and reduces entrepreneurial action.** The majority of survey participants choose pure exploitation, a proxy for strategic management, as their response when disruptive business models are introduced into their industry. This further validates the view that business school education and the past generation (or two or three)

of business managers have focused on strategic management as a response to adverse change in the environment.

4. **Threat-rigid responses to critical threats reduce entrepreneurial action.** We tested two distinct forms of threat – performance reducing (i.e., the belief that the disruption will reduce sales and growth) and critical (i.e., the belief that the disruption could put you out of business). Interestingly, managers are motivated to act in the face of performance reduction but tend to freeze up – or respond in a "threat-rigid" manner – when facing critical threat.

5. **Vision and implied predictability drive entrepreneurial action.** Managers need confidence that they can plot a specific path forward to establish a sense of predictability. Predictability, and a vision of the future state of the organization, are among the most powerful forces in driving intentions to consider profound organizational change such as adopting a disruptive business model.

6. **Urgency is a friend, or foe, to entrepreneurial action.** A certain amount of time pressure works, but too much time pressure causes a threat-rigid response. John Kotter, one of the gurus of change management, identified urgency as one of the primary drivers of change, and our research supported this. But we also found that urgency only works up to a point, beyond which, if the time is seen as too short to turn the ship around, managers become threat-rigid and resign themselves to going down with the ship.

These findings were valuable in understanding the mindset of strategic decision-makers who face challenging times when disruption threatens a previously fruitful business. These findings, along with advanced research on motivation theory, have been combined to develop a motivation model of entrepreneurial thinking.

A Motivation Model of Entrepreneurial Thinking

Other researchers have blazed a path for us to identify the antecedents of entrepreneurial thought. Collectively, these findings help knit together the connections that will lead to a better understanding of how to create an entrepreneurial firm where one currently does not exist. An overview of two dominant paths of research in this area is provided below, and then pulled together with our research findings to develop a new construct, grounded in motivational theory, which we call entrepreneurial thinking.

Duane Ireland, Michael Hitt, and David Sirmon, co-founders of the strategic entrepreneurship school, have identified four specific dimensions to strategic entrepreneurship: (1) an entrepreneurial mindset, (2) entrepreneurial culture and leadership, (3) strategic management of resources, and (4) the ability to apply creativity and develop innovation.[5] These dimensions have been tested for more than a decade and have been applied extensively in research by scholars attempting to further the topics of strategic entrepreneurship, corporate entrepreneurship, and opportunity discovery and creation.

Another rich field of academic study that I incorporate into the model is entrepreneurial orientation, which involves assessing the firm's orientation toward entrepreneurial solutions. Recognizing the earlier point that strategic management already has the most powerful seat at the boardroom table, many scholars have focused exclusively on understanding how to promote entrepreneurial action. Entrepreneurial orientation is valuable as an effective measure of a firm's entrepreneurial capabilities. This entails assessing five key antecedents: (1) autonomy, (2) innovativeness, (3) risk taking, (4) proactiveness, and (5) competitive aggressiveness.[6]

Having combined these three distinct yet interrelated streams of research findings, we can see clear relationships and similarities. Each of the research streams identifies the importance of opportunity discovery or creation, innovation, and risk-taking. Strategic entrepreneurship focuses on the individual mindset and the organizational culture, while entrepreneurial orientation is more specific with respect to a need for autonomy, proactiveness, and competitive aggressiveness. Our research supports the strategic entrepreneurship dimension of leadership and effective resource management.

Table 6.2 maps these findings against the three core constructs of Icek Ajzen's theory of planned behavior.[7] It indicates that much of

Table 6.2 Mapping theories of entrepreneurial action onto motivation theory

Motivation theory (Ajzen, 1991)	Entrepreneurial response to disruption (Dewald and Osiyevskyy, 2011–2015)	Strategic entrepreneurship (Ireland, Hitt, and Sirmon, 2003)	Entrepreneurial orientation (Dess and Lumpkin, 2005)	Motivational theory that precedes entrepreneurial thinking
Behavioral beliefs – the individual believes that intended actions will lead to intended results	Opportunity identification, positive risk experience	Entrepreneurial mindset, applying creativity and developing innovation	Innovativeness, proactiveness	A belief that opportunities can be discovered or created
Normative beliefs – the belief that important people support the intended actions	Strategic management domination and critical threat response	Entrepreneurial culture and leadership	Autonomy, risk taking	A belief that an entrepreneur-driven organization culture drives exploration
Control beliefs – the belief that the intended actions can be taken on and completed	Vision and predictability, urgency	Managing resources strategically	Competitive aggressiveness	A belief in the ability to achieve entrepreneurial outcomes through action

the work done to understand how firms can adopt a more entrepreneurial perspective fits well into the Ajzen model, which represents the antecedents of motivational intentions and entrepreneurial actions. This process is inductive and hence somewhat speculative, but nevertheless valuable as an entrepreneurial exercise in recombination and explorative study. Let me provide more context for each variable.

I feel like I am throwing a lot at you with not much explanation. Let me back up and walk through each of Ajzen's belief propositions and how they apply to each of the entrepreneurial response, strategic entrepreneurship, and entrepreneurial orientation frameworks.

Ajzen's theory of planned behavior is used to explain why some people are motivated to take on challenging tasks (such as losing weight, fulfilling an exercise program, or stopping smoking), while others are not. This addresses only one element – the situational dimension – of such decisions. There are also dispositional characteristics (i.e., some people simply do not have the ability to change). Azjen's theory relies on three fundamental beliefs that drive decision-making intentions and action; behavioral, normative, and control.

Behavioral belief is the belief that a specific action will have intended results. To put it perhaps too simply, people who believe they will be healthier and live longer and better lives if they stop smoking or start exercising or lose weight are much more likely to formulate intentions and engage in actions to support those beliefs. Looking at the argument in the negative, a person who does not believe that smoking is harmful to their body and is shortening their life span is highly unlikely to go through the short-term pain of quitting smoking in the hope of a possible long-term payoff. In the literature, this variable is also referred to and measured as "attitude."

The decision-maker's attitude reflects a belief that the behavior will (or will not) result in specific benefits. When considering decision-making for the firm, strategic decision-makers may refuse to accept the possibility that opportunities are discovered or created by individuals in the organization. This attitude is grounded in a specific behavioral belief, and as one can readily see, it is unlikely that resources will be allocated toward high-risk entrepreneurial actions when the strategic decision-maker's behavioral belief is that doing so will not benefit the firm.

You may have experienced the operationalization of a negative attitude in your place of business. Perhaps creative thought is assumed to be the exclusive domain of certain people, such as those in marketing or research. When leaders feel that opportunities are not discovered or created, organizations tend to grow bureaucratic systems that eschew the thought of creativity from within the regular ranks, or even among the leaders of operating units. Such organizations set out to keep employees focused on the task in front of them and do not allow them to "daydream" or waste precious operational time seeking new opportunities. This "stick to it" mindset is counter to the entrepreneurial thinking attitude of seeking opportunities and innovativeness at all levels of the organization.

An entrepreneurial mindset – proactiveness, along with the ability to apply creativity and develop innovation – reflects the attitude that opportunities can be created or discovered. Furthermore, prior positive risk experience drives entrepreneurial action, thereby reinforcing the attitude that opportunities can be discovered and created by members of the firm.

Normative beliefs represent the collective viewpoints of people who have a significant influence in our lives. For instance, you may not be sure that lack of exercise will harm your life, but if it is important to your spouse or children, or your boss or team members, then your chances of starting to exercise will increase. Ajzen describes normative beliefs as attending to subjective norms imposed by "important" people (meaning those whom the individual sees as important). In an organization context, subjective norms are generally established and reinforced through the culture of the organization. Ireland and colleagues focus quite a bit of their framework discussion on organizational culture, stating that "an effective entrepreneurial culture is one in which new ideas and creativity are expected, risk taking is encouraged, failure is tolerated, learning is promoted, product, process and administrative innovations are championed, and continuous change is viewed as a conveyor of opportunities."[8]

Ireland and colleagues' description of an entrepreneurial organizational culture is in stark contrast to what Oleksiy Osiyevskyy
and I found in our research to be the dominant organization culture,
whether the organization is a small, private, and owner-operated
firm or a large, sophisticated, and publicly funded one. To be honest, what I have observed in my past business experience and in
my travels to corporate offices does not reflect the learning, exploring, open culture depicted by Ireland's team. Generally, corporate
culture reflects the dominant paradigm of strategic management –
that is, critical threats lead to threat-rigid responses and ducking for
cover rather than risk taking, learning, and innovation. Dess and
Lumpkin respond to this reality by adding the need for autonomy
and risk-taking as measures of entrepreneurial orientation that represent effective entrepreneurial organization culture.

The third belief Ajzen identified is the control belief, more commonly known as perceived behavioral control. Notice that he categorizes
behavioral control as "perceived." In other words, the motivation to
take action is driven more by the perception that you can control
the behavior or action than by an objectively measured realization
of such control. Using weight loss as an example, perceived behavioral control represents the individual's belief that s/he has the
willpower and intestinal fortitude to take the steps to lose weight.
Many behavioral trends starts well but flicker out in the absence of
perceived behavioral control. This explains why fitness clubs sell
lifetime memberships; they fully anticipate that most of their new
customers will not actually have the drive to keep coming after a
few sessions. This very specific circumstance marries the business
model belief that people do not have the behavioral control they
perceive, with the individual's hope that by paying for a lifetime
membership, they will move their behavioral control from perception to reality. Rather poetic, with an entrepreneurial outcome.

Leadership and past performance are key to building the perception that the organization can and will follow through on entrepreneurial actions. Within this category, I include our findings on
urgency, which is arguably a perception that can be managed within
the organization, along with predictability, vision, and competitive

aggressiveness. In related research, Oleksiy and his colleagues found that entrepreneurial ventures with inspiring visions of the future attract growth support much more quickly than other ventures. The more connected the vision is to an actionable marketing plan, the more salient the growth influence. This confirms the perceptive importance of behavioral control.[9]

These factors together amount to a motivational theory of entrepreneurial action that is a foundation for entrepreneurial thinking: (1) a strong belief that opportunities can be discovered or created from within the unit or organization, (2) an organizational culture that supports entrepreneurial action, and (3) a shared belief that the organization has the ability to execute its entrepreneurial actions.

Chapter Summary

The main messages in this chapter are:

1 Recent research into the micro-foundations of decision-making has provided a roadmap for better understanding the antecedents of corporate entrepreneurship.
2 The three main elements of motivation theory that drive entrepreneurial thinking are:
   (a) the belief that specific actions can lead to opportunity discovery and creation, which then leads to entrepreneurial actions and sustained wealth creation for the firm,
   (b) the belief that an effective organizational culture can support and drive entrepreneurial actions, and
   (c) the shared belief that the organization has the ability to execute on its entrepreneurial actions.
3 In contrast to more common critical thinking and other reductionist rational thinking models, entrepreneurial thinking expands the firm's horizon of growth and wealth creation opportunities.

7 Creating the Entrepreneurial Organization

Culture eats strategy for breakfast

Peter Drucker[1]

Where do great ideas come from? For me, one of the most troubling aspects of creativity and opportunity seeking is that there are so many who believe that there are only a few creative people and then there are the rest of us. Poppycock. Well, in fairness, there are certainly some people who are more creative than the norm, but if we want firms to develop and exploit entrepreneurial opportunities, the first step to recognize that opportunities are not the exclusive domain of a few creative people. Opportunities come from everyday people, and it is up to management to use proven systems and processes to support opportunity development.

Imagine being a municipal transportation planner in a room of municipal managers. There is the budget officer, the communications manager, the engineer, and so on. The politicians are looking for someone's head because their constituents are reporting poorly sequenced traffic lights (yes, seemingly silly, but many a senior manager has lost his or her job over lesser political issues). The councilor recounts the phone call received from a constituent: "I will not wait through another red light at Home Road when there is absolutely no traffic going through on the crossroad that has the green light.

Why do you only hire idiots as engineers and planners – can't they sequence the lights so I won't have to be inconvenienced when I have important business to tend to? I want someone's head and I want the lights fixed once and for all!"

Back in the boardroom, the frustration sets in. The politician is concerned about losing votes if the concerned constituent goes to the newspaper with her complaint. The planner says that people should be encouraged to take public transit to save the environment and create more vibrant communities, and then the city will operate more efficiently and beneficially for all. The engineer says that if further studies were completed he could more accurately estimate traffic loadings and install timers to shift the sequencing every hour, or for that matter every ten minutes. It is simply a matter of having the resources to do the study and analysis – it is a matter of committing the budget. The budget officer says she can allocate the money, but that would cause a deficit, which means there would need to be an increase in taxes, at which point the politician barks out, "No bloody way, I am not losing my job because of tax increases!"

In the silence of frustration, an aide says, "Wouldn't it be great if the traffic could tell the lights to turn green?" Ha ha – everyone laughs.

But then the engineer says, "I never thought of the problem that way. We could look into ways to build advanced indicators that recognize when vehicles are coming up to the intersection." Presto, like magic the seeds of an opportunity are born. This discussion then leads to the development of electronic indicators placed into pavement, which in fact is what is now commonly used to communicate to the lights that it is time to change from red to green.

While this is just a fictitious story, I am hoping you can see the potential of putting together a group of people who would not normally consider themselves "creative," but who nevertheless struggle with a problem until a shift comes about that presents the problem in a new light, thereby introducing a potential new opportunity.

Sadly, not all organizations hold interdisciplinary meetings and discussions. What does it take to be a truly entrepreneurial organization? The analysis in the previous chapter led to a motivational framework for entrepreneurial thinking that engages (1) opportunity identification, (2) a supportive entrepreneurial organizational culture, and (3) an ability to fulfill entrepreneurial initiatives. Those three elements have been sequenced in that order to match the flow for a specific entrepreneurial action (which starts with an opportunity/idea, is nurtured within a supportive entrepreneurial culture, and is implemented through an entrepreneurial process). But from a long-term perspective, corporations need to first establish and nurture an entrepreneurial culture, so this chapter is organized first to describe the elements of an entrepreneurially supportive organizational culture, then to discuss where opportunities come from, and finally to outline a process whereby opportunities can be developed and enacted in the marketplace.

An Entrepreneurial Culture

One of the most heartwarming accounts of entrepreneurial culture has to be Brett Wilson's story of the founding of First Energy Capital Corp. In *Redefining Success: Still Making Mistakes*,[2] Wilson describes how four entrepreneurs who were young and enthusiastic, and underexperienced but wise, entered the high-stakes and *über*-competitive industry of corporate finance. What was their cloak of protection? Wilson speaks of establishing a highly values-driven culture in which integrity was paramount, relationships were sacred, and the team relied on respecting and depending on the unique strengths of each partner. Their organizational culture and commitment to organizational values became a source of differentiation that led to the firm's phenomenal success.

Whether it relates to a start-up or a corporate venture, fostering and nurturing an entrepreneurial organizational culture is a common thread in virtually all entrepreneurship theories. Every organizational culture is distinct and largely unique, but there are some models that managers can use as guides for adjusting or revamping an organization to drive an entrepreneurial spirit. With corporate ventures, as noted earlier, there is much at stake and far more

administrative heritage and institutional memory, and this can overwhelm and hold back entrepreneurial genius. So I will be employing
a four-point framework for assessing corporate culture: (1) a clear
narrative of entrepreneurial success within the firm, (2) acceptance
of failure, (3) the promotion and rewarding of learning, and (4) risk
taking that is supported but also contained in its potential impact
(i.e., don't bet the farm, at least not with every new idea). *What* is one
thing, but *how* is quite another.

One approach to developing an entrepreneurial culture is to start
with a clear narrative of entrepreneurial success. The seven stories
framework developed by Martin and colleagues[3] offers one effective means to help organizations establish a reliable and consistent
organizational culture. It focuses on narratives related to the cultural
dimensions of equality, security, and control. Table 7.1 summarizes
the seven stories.

While descriptive, this framework is useful because it encompasses the diversity of organizational cultures, all of which have their
idiosyncrasies. The first group of three questions relates to how
egalitarian the organizational culture is. Are the rules for big bosses
the same as for the common employee? Can the common person
ever rise to the top? When applying this to an entrepreneurial culture, the results should point to a highly egalitarian and transpar-
ent organization. Staff members should feel comfortable asking the
boss questions and pointing out rule-breaking in the spirit of learning (not in an accusatory manner). The boss should be seen as human, if not equal to all team members, and it should be completely
plausible that any team member with the necessary skills and abilities can rise to the top.

The second group of questions relates to the level of security and
support the employee can expect from the firm. Is loyalty reciprocal
and justified? Finally, the last question is of primary importance to
entrepreneurial spirit and drive: How restricted is the control within the organization – or, more positively, how much freedom does
the employee have to pursue new initiatives? Research on what is
needed to foster an entrepreneurial culture consistently emphasizes

Table 7.1 Concerns underlying common concerns in organizational stories

Concerns	Specifics (adapted slightly to fit the 21st-century workplace)	Entrepreneurial culture
quality versus equality	What do I do when a higher-status person breaks a rule?	Talk to them – the culture must be transparent and open.
	Is the big boss human?	Yes, and even seen as an equal.
	Can the little person rise to the top?	Definitely, with the right skills and abilities.
security versus security	Will I be laid off?	Only as a last resort – entrepreneurial firms are dedicated to their employees.
	Will the organization help me when I am in need personally?	Definitely, entrepreneurial organizations care for their team members.
	How will the boss react to mistakes (or failure)?	Failures are encouraged, and present opportunities for learning.
control versus lack of control	How will the organization deal with external obstacles?	The entrepreneurial firm provides autonomy for its team members, and is proactive in supporting them.

the need for autonomy supported by proactiveness on the part of the organization's employees *and* leaders.

Entrepreneurial organizations require risk-taking and bold initiatives. This is best narrated through stories that demonstrate equality, security, and lack of control. Robots & Pencils (R&P) is a radical new firm dedicated to building mobile apps – not a unique business in the twenty-first century. This firm has a very unique entrepreneurial culture. In five years, R&P has attracted 77 million users across 169 countries and has been featured in the *Wall Street Journal*, the *New York Times*, and *Wired* and on ZDNet.

Michael Sikorsky, the CEO of R&P, has developed an organizational culture that starts with a deep respect for the distinctiveness of each employee. All have unique talents that they bring to the table. R&P's creed is: "Everything we do starts by blending the sciences with the humanities – the robots with the pencils – the programmers with the designers."[4]

Sikorsky is very casual and open, presenting himself much more as an equal to the other team members than as someone with special status. How should employees respond when he breaks a rule? Call him on it, of course, but then don't be surprised if he gives a good reason for breaking the rule. This is more about asking "Why is there this rule?" than about sending a message that it is fine to break rules (what few there might be). The point is for the team members to be respectful of one another and to stay focused on creating new apps, not following a bunch of rules. Michael also makes it clear that if they want, anyone can rise to the top (which isn't far from where he resides). This sort of equality is demonstrated in other ways, such as by sharing financial benefits.

As with most twenty-first-century organizations, personal support is a given. Probably the most impactful component of Sikorsky's magic cultural cocktail is how he treats failure. As he puts it, "fail early, fail fast." What happens when an R&P project fails? First, within R&P there are layers of mitigation aimed at celebrating the fail early and avoiding catastrophic failures. For starters, there are no project-specific budgets, because that would saddle one particular person with a failure, and just like success, failure is a team responsibility. As noted on the R&P website: "Our robots and pencils love building apps, and are motivated to create code and art that stands apart. Our developers are encouraged to think of novel and unconventional approaches to programming challenges. Our artists take the same approach to design."

When the robots or pencils feel that a new app is not a clear winner, R&P has the most creative way of beta testing – they promote the new app under another name – let's test it out! If it flies, then bring it under the corporate banner, but until then let the market have at it. Again, this protects all project participants from the scars of failure.

Jim Whitehurst, CEO of Red Hat, recently authored *The Open Organization: Igniting Passion and Performance*.[5] Whitehurst views Red Hat as an exemplary open organization, in that it is structured around addressing *why* (which ignites passion through motivation and inspiration), then *how* (meritocracy and getting things done), and then *what* (catalyzing inclusive decision-making). This order is opposite to what Whitehurst observes in conventional organizations, where the senior leadership starts with *what*, which drives *how*, and where *why* is represented by individual promotion and pay. Whitehurst's emphasis on *why* as a starting point reflects the excellent work done by Simon Sinek and shared in his best-seller *Start with Why: How Great Leaders Inspire Everyone to Take Action.*[6] In short, members of an organization need to understand why, that is, the purpose of their work, in order to feel inspired to share in the firm's innovation, growth, and entrepreneurial transformation.

Organizational culture can also be adjusted through specific perspectives, values, and norms. In a way, this amounts to reverse engineering of a desired narrative in that it endorses specific actions that will ultimately build to the creation of a clear narrative of organizational behavior. Following are three transformative approaches that engage individuals by endorsing behaviors and perspectives that lead to an entrepreneurial culture.

Time perspectives. Philip Zimbardo, the Stanford psychology professor who ran the controversial Stanford prison experiment in 1971, developed a thorough understanding of why good people can still do bad things. In the process, he discovered that there is a seemingly benign but highly instructive antecedent to behaviors, which he termed time perspective.[7] The argument goes that people have one of three primary time perspectives: past, present, and future. Each of these can have a positive or negative orientation; thus, there are six perspectives in all.

With the *past-positive* perspective, the past is "half-full." For example, seeing or hearing children, and certain smells like baked cookies, bring back fond memories, possibly even overwhelming joy. People with a past-positive perspective are variously described as warm, sentimental, friendly, happy, self-confident, and seldom anxious, depressed, or aggressive.[8] Past-positive people, who are comfortable with the status quo, are very important to an organization in terms of supporting the positive attitude of people who are facing difficult situations. Entrepreneurial organizations tend to challenge the status quo, but because the orientation of the past-positive perspective is positive versus negative (as opposed to good versus bad), and such people always want to be on the positive side, the past-positive orientation is critical to developing an entrepreneurial culture.

In contrast, the *past-negative* perspective can be linked to reclusive, almost isolated people who regret past actions and long for the opportunity to change the past (which of course is impossible). They may be described as unhappy, depressed, anxious, shy, and at times frustrated and prone to lose their temper quickly. Past-negative perspectives can impede the development of an entrepreneurial culture.

The *present-positive* perspective – or as Zimbardo terms it, "present-hedonistic" – is all about following the pleasure principle: I want it now, I want it all, and so on, in embrace of the creed, "If it feels good, do it!" The positive-hedonistic person is adventurous, fun loving, and highly risk-prone. In a successful entrepreneurial culture, an element of positive-hedonism is definitely helpful, in that it encourages risk-taking perspectives. But caution must be exercised to resist betting the farm.

The *present-negative* or "present-fatalistic" time perspective reflects an absence of personal efficacy, which can lead to anxiety, unhappiness, apathy, and even depression. Present-fatalistic individuals can be high in risk-taking, but not because they believe in rolling the dice in hopes of a big win; rather, they don't believe that anything will make a difference or make life better. For these people, risk-taking is just another way of proving that nothing matters.

Future perspective is not so much positive or negative; it has more to do with reality versus a transcendental orientation. The *reality principle* is reflective of planning, that is, it seeks a trade-off between instant gratification and uncertain but potentially more significant future benefits. Future-perspective individuals are described as extremely conscientious, consistent, and concerned about future consequences. They organize themselves with to-do lists, they complete their work on time (or ahead of schedule), and they believe that hard work will be rewarded.

The *transcendental-future perspective* represents the view that life on earth is merely a path to an after-death experience. Individuals with a predominant transcendental-future perspective have good impulse control, are not aggressive, and are concerned about the future consequences of present choices and actions.

The future perspective brings to mind another Stanford experiment known as the Stanford marshmallow experiment. Walter Mischel and Ebbe Ebbesen gave young children aged four to six the option of having one marshmallow now, or waiting fifteen minutes (alone with the one marshmallow) and receiving a reward of two Oreo cookies if they did not eat the marshmallow. This was, of course, an impossible task for most children. Here is the kicker (and this is big – get ready). The researchers reconnected with the children years later, when they were eighteen. The children who demonstrated the future-oriented ability to delay gratification scored, on average, 210 points higher on verbal and math SAT scores. Mischel reported that delayed gratification at age four was a better predictor of SAT scores than IQ![9] The post-study also found that the children who could wait for the delayed gratification had developed what Zimbardo had described as "a range of superior emotional and social competencies" and "were better able to deal with adversity and stress, and they were more self-confident, diligent, and self-reliant."[10]

Zimbardo and Boyd identified a blend of time perspectives as optimal in the Western world:

• High in past-positive time perspective
• Moderately high in future time perspective
• Moderately high in present-hedonistic time perspective
• Low in past-negative time perspective
• Low in present-fatalistic time perspective[11]

In terms of entrepreneurial culture, the organization has the opportunity to blend various time perspectives by establishing organizational values and a clear narrative that embraces the blend of time perspectives recommended by Zimbardo and Boyd. As a forward-looking organization, an entrepreneurial culture may require a stronger emphasis on future time perspective.

Positivity. Key to time perspective research is the distinction between a positive and a negative perspective. According to Barbara Fredrickson, a psychologist at UNC–Chapel Hill, positivity is not fatalistic or predetermined, but a conscious choice.[12] Her research has done much to help us understand that individuals can *choose* a positive or negative framing of the time perspective (something that Zimbardo and Boyd also argue). Psychologists generally agree that positivity and time perspective can be adjusted through hard work and thoughtful practice.

Growth mindsets. In *Mindset*,[13] Carol Dweck of Stanford University differentiates between fixed and growth mindsets and discusses how individuals can pursue a growth mindset.

These ideas can be combined to help build the core elements of an entrepreneurial organizational culture from the people up. Organizations need to (1) know the time perspective, positivity, and growth mindset of key people in the organization, and (2) develop tools to refine the positive growth orientation of organizational leaders and members. To be sure, diversity is essential. Nevertheless, as Jim Collins argues in *Good to Great*, it is vital to get the "right people on the bus," which in the present context means selecting people with a past-positive, present-hedonistic, or future time perspective, then vigilantly developing positivity and growth mindsets to create an organizational culture that is rich in the spirit of entrepreneurial enthusiasm.

Start with an Opportunity

There is a rising debate in academic circles regarding whether opportunities are discovered or created. Let me put it another way – are opportunities just sitting out there waiting to be discovered, or do entrepreneurs create opportunities out of thin air? Let's explore this question by considering a modern exemplar of corporate entrepreneurship: Apple. Were the opportunities there for the taking, or did Apple create them from thin air?

Steve Jobs himself engaged Walter Isaacson to write his biography. The result, simply called *Steve Jobs*,[14] is a revealing and insightful description of the larger-than-life former Apple CEO and the evolution of Apple. Relying largely on Isaacson's research, let's look at the main products developed by Apple and Jobs:

1 The personal desktop computer (Apple I): Arguably, Apple *created* the personal computer market at a time when people could not really get their heads around the idea of combining an electronic typewriter with a game console and a calculator.
2 The Macintosh: This largely entailed *discovery* of the gap between what the personal desktop computers of the day were offering and what the customer was starting to see as their potential.
3 The iMac: This computer with an integrated monitor and keyboard (but without a floppy disk slot) was a step forward in convenience and style that was again a *discovery* of a missing link for existing customers.
4 iTunes: This was clearly a *discovery* in that it served to replace the illegal pirating of music.
5 iPod: While there was an element of discovery in this, I weigh in on the *creation* side, for the iPod was a unique device that celebrated a new age in music listening – 1,000 songs in a small box, white earphones, a one-disc tool for accessing content, and so on. A truly amazing advance in industrial design.
6 iPhone: This was a *discovery* of the somewhat predictable merging of smartphones, the iPod, the camera, and so on.
7 iPad: We're back to *creation*, in that there was clearly no market for tablets (or at least only a struggling market for earlier attempts). Indeed, the iPad is interesting because of the many predictions of failure for what seemed to be an inferior computer that would not support plug-ins, printers, common software such as word processing, and the like.

OK, I guess this didn't provide much clarity. Which might cause you to ask, "Does it really matter whether an opportunity is discovered or created?"

From a learning and development perspective, this question is important. If opportunities are primarily *discovered*, then a firm seeking to succeed at corporate entrepreneurship should focus its training, resources, and energy on scanning the marketplace for unexploited or underexploited opportunities. On the other hand, if opportunities are *created*, then the firm should focus more on research and development, generating products or services that can create demand. The evidence from Apple suggests a need to develop capabilities both to discover and to create. But then, we must consider the model itself – few if any organizations have the potential to be the next Apple. How do firms focus on developing capabilities that will drive them forward in either opportunity discovery or in opportunity creation, and ultimately in both?

To be sure, entrepreneurial ventures are born every day, and the evidence indicates that opportunities are discovered, *and* they are created, *and* at times they are a blurry combination of both discovery and creation. Firms that desire to become more entrepreneurial need to grasp the importance of the distinction and be purposeful in supporting the necessary paths to both.

Opportunity Discovery

Market intelligence is king in the world of opportunity discovery. But when I say market, I mean much more than the customer market. I mean markets in an all-encompassing sense that includes supply markets, sales markets, complementary markets, and even unrelated markets.

In 2005, W. Chan Kim and Renée Mauborgne of INSEAD Business School authored a ground-shaking business book titled *Blue Ocean Strategy: How to Create Uncontested Market Space and Make the Competition Irrelevant*.[15] A key component of the Blue Ocean thesis is opportunity discovery. The authors provide a framework, referred to as the six paths to find new market space. Those paths entail exploration across (1) alternative industries, (2) strategic groups, (3) customers, (4) complementary offerings, (5) functional or emotional appeal, and (6) timelines.

By exploring and adopting practices from alternative industries, firms can discover new ways to approach customer needs. For example, Southwest Airlines examined bus and private car transportation alternatives to identify key elements of the Southwest discount point-to-point model. This led to it becoming the largest airline in the world (as determined by market capitalization).

Strategic grouping distinguishes product or service offerings within a specific industry. For instance, management consulting can come in the form of a single proprietor (as a member of a single proprietor strategic group) or a multinational such as McKinsey or BCG. In both cases the firm receives management consulting, and without distinguishing the quality of each, there are significant differences in resource capabilities, scope of services, multi-location offerings, and so on. Consider the beer industry, which has strategic groups ranging from micro-breweries to global giants Anheuser-Busch InBev and SABMiller. Consumers buy beer from each, but in terms of brewing, bottling, distribution, sales, advertising, and so on, they are radically difference businesses.

Without walking through each of the categories, it is important to note that Kim and Mauborgne's six-path framework provides a great starting point for firms that are looking outside the box for that "indicator in the pavement" form of break-through opportunity. This systematic approach to discovering opportunities can be adopted by any firm in any industry.

When I present some of these ideas, people are always astounded that discovering opportunities can actually be a highly planned and purposeful corporate action. It is simply a matter of prioritizing, setting aside the always present tasks of the day, pulling together an interdisciplinary team, giving them the encouragement and freedom to explore ways to do things differently, and providing them with tools and processes to start discovering.

Another powerful tool Kim and Mauborgne recommend for discovering opportunities is the strategy canvas – again, a highly purposeful tool that plots the attributes that drive buyer action against customer perceptions of each competitor's specific offering. Once the canvas is developed, management is challenged to identify factors that can be eliminated, reduced, raised, or created. This finessing was applied in our business school as a tool to fine-tune our MBA offering, and was instrumental in developing new opportunities that have increased enrolments and student satisfaction.

Sometimes opportunities are discovered accidentally. For instance, Clayton Christensen often includes a story in his presentations that focuses on the entrepreneur's need to understand the "job to be done" as a means to better understand and exploit market opportunities.[16] Christensen was brought in as a consultant by a quick service restaurant (QSR) that could not understand why milkshake sales in the early morning hours had suddenly exploded. The firm wanted to ensure it had thoroughly captured the market – was there a certain flavour that would be the most attractive? The QSR had followed its standard protocol for analysis, which started with customer demographics: age, income level, marital status, number of children, and so on.

Christensen approached the situation somewhat differently: his first question was not who or what, but *why*? Why were people buying milkshakes at 6 a.m.? What "job" was the milkshake doing? What was the source of fulfillment?

What he discovered was that early morning commuters could not rely on coffee to keep them awake on their early morning commute. Coffee was too hot at first, and then quickly cooled and went stale. Milkshakes, by contrast, are thick and viscous, requiring concentration and intense suction on the straw, and this kept the driver alert. A milkshake was also cold to the touch, which kept people awake, and it took twenty to thirty minutes to drink, which was just the right time for a commute. The job to be done was nourishing the driver while keeping him or her alert through a morning commute. An opportunity had been discovered somewhat by accident.

Academic researchers have offered a number of formal methods – including communities of practice, communities of creation, and organizational learning – for generating ideas and inventions that can lead to innovation and induced strategic actions. Motivation theory drives home the importance of a positive attitude toward intended actions, and a deep body of research on both internally generated and externally observed opportunities indicates that opportunity discovery is a fundamental first stage in the pursuit of entrepreneurial thinking.

I end this section by passing on a word about the best-known process for opportunity discovery: brainstorming. Brainstorming absolutely works, but only if its core rules are followed strictly. I list them below:

- As the facilitator, practice independence (better yet, hire an independent facilitator).
- Do not criticize!
- Use a flip chart (yes, a flip chart – the paper and activity of writing is important) and accurately record output (don't screen what you think is relevant, but instead check with the participant to ensure you have fully captured their point).
- Encourage piggybacking, and generally maintain a positive, expansive atmosphere.
- Do not evaluate – that can be done later.

Opportunity Creation

Creating opportunities from scratch is more often tied to the firm's resource base – more specifically, to R&D, new product or service development, and engineering. Opportunities are created by developing new products or services that reflect what customers will want, not what they seek today. In support of this approach, Michael Sikorsky of R&P argues that planning is an important component of opportunity creation that must be taken seriously and pursued with diligence. It is instructive here to quote Sir Winston Churchill: "Plans are of little importance, but planning is essential."

When creating opportunities, it is essential to make plans and look toward the future. Of course, the risk quotient will be much higher for opportunity creation because the entrepreneur is presenting something completely new to what is often not an existing customer but a forecasted one. But the reward can be much greater if the effort succeeds. Opportunity creation more accurately reflects the romantic vision of entrepreneurial genius – the garage entrepreneur who creates a great invention that everyone just has to have.

Opportunity creation connects more directly with conventional theories of invention leading to innovation. Invention is the creation of something new; innovation is the commercialization of that invention. Invention was creating the stickiness that led to the innovation of 3M Post-its. Invention is the internal combustion engine, which led to the innovation of cars, motorcycles, lawn mowers, airplanes, and so on. This is the traditional world of patents and systematic invention leading to innovation paths – the world so often encountered in any textbook on innovation. Some refer to this as the "push" approach to innovation, in the sense that the invention pushes the idea into a marketable innovation.

Causation, Effectuation, and Bricolage

Entrepreneurship scholars have differentiated three processes by which entrepreneurs pursue their initiatives and ideas. Causal reasoning is analogous to the critical thinking paradigm described earlier. Under causal reasoning, the entrepreneur seemingly has a clear prediction of outcomes resulting from inputs, and hence sets a clear goal that can be achieved through predictable means. This approach is highly theoretical and rooted in predictability and certainty. The entrepreneur identifies alternative means of achieving a given goal and then, as with critical thinking, selects the best path forward. Essentially, causation is about having a clearly defined goal and selecting a path for achieving that goal from among alternatives. But causation has recently been widely discounted by empirical researchers, so it is appropriate to focus more on the two remaining processes.

Effectuation and bricolage approaches to thinking and decision-making turn the rational strategic management paradigm on its head. In his seminal research, Sara Sarasvathy[17] of the Darden School of Business has correctly pointed out that the traditional causation approach (from objectives to means) in entrepreneurial settings is usually substituted by its alternative, effectuation, which presupposes going from a set of available means to a set of aspirations. According to Sarasvathy, causation focuses on making effective predictions of an uncertain future, whereas effectuation focuses on leveraging the controllable aspects of an unpredictable future. Hence, effectuation is most effective for creating new markets (strategic entrepreneurship), whereas causation may be more appropriate for exploiting existing markets through competitive strategies.

Stepping out of the academic jargon, you probably know effectuation better by the term "lean," as in lean start-up. Eric Reis authored the book *The Lean Startup: How Constant Innovation Creates Radically Successful Businesses*. The more descriptive pattern demonstrated by Reis is an extension of Peters and Waterman's "Ready–Fire–Aim" framework. Reis prefers the framework of "Vision–Steer–Accelerate." Reis's book was closely followed by Remy Arteaga and Joanne Hyland's *Pivot: How Top Entrepreneurs Adapt and Change Course to Find Ultimate Success*. In their book, Arteaga and Hyland present their own three-stage process, which they refer to as "Plant–Pivot–Propel," which they acknowledge was inspired by and based on the Rensselaer Polytechnic Institute framework of "Discovery–Incubation–Acceleration."

I recommend that entrepreneurs, be they individual or corporate, familiarize themselves with each of these frameworks as means to better understand and implement the core elements of envisioning/planning an entrepreneurial initiative, followed by action that is fungible and readily adjusted to meet market needs (or able to find a new market), and followed then by fast action.

Bricolage is a relatively new concept in management literature, drawn from French anthropologist Claude Lévi-Strauss's *The Savage*

Mind.[18] In management studies, bricolage can be best described as "making do with what one has" to meet a customer need. In a way, bricolage is at the far end of a continuum that has detailed analysis at the other end.

The poster child for bricolage is that well-known fix-it man, MacGyver (from TV fame) – a little of this, a little of that, some duct tape, and presto, a transistor radio (or a bomb), whatever is needed to solve the problem. For another example, picture the movie *Apollo 13*, in the scene where the NASA supervisor throws a bunch of spaceship parts on a table and tells the team, "Build an air exchanger."[19] The engineers are dazed and confused, but by applying bricolage, they develop an air exchanger and are able to explain an assembly protocol that saves the lives of three astronauts in space. Bricolage represents unknown means but known predetermined outcomes.

Bricolage can be a really inspiring way to motivate innovation. My sense after reading Walter Isaacson's biography of Steve Jobs was that the Apple co-founder was a bricoleur at heart. He knew what he wanted but did not know how to get there. Every day in the Apple research labs must have been like that intense two hours for the Apollo 13 engineers – make it work or someone is not going to make it (i.e., someone or maybe all of you will be dropped from the team). Jobs epitomized the inspiring leader who has a clear sense of the end target but needs someone, a team, group of bricoleurs, to fill in the middle. This is bricolage at its finest.

Another amazing modern-day example of bricolage is the brainchild of Peter Diamindis, who created and is chair and CEO of the XPrize Foundation. The XPrize foundation provides large financial prizes for open competitions that address bold and audacious goals. The most famous was space travel: the XPrize was $10 million for a manned independent flight vehicle capable of safely taking three people 100 kilometers above the Earth's surface (and back) twice within two weeks. This was an inspirational and achievable vision that entailed limited resources, limited time, and unknown means.

By comparison, the effectuation process has largely been used to describe human relations and processes involving strategic relationships, affordable loss, and the exploiting of contingencies. Effectuation is generally tied to a resource-rich environment (not money, but accomplished scientists, effective discovery processes, etc.), whereas bricolage is generally tied to strong leadership and a vision of a new future for the firm.

In a way, bricolage mirrors effectuation with respect to organizational resources and exploiting opportunities and resolving problems using existing available resources. Note that effectuation and bricolage are complements to rather than substitutes for traditional rational approaches to thinking (their counterparts are causation and optimization, respectively). As researchers, including Sarasvathy, have demonstrated, each approach is applicable in certain circumstances, and neither can be presumed to be the only right way.

The study of causation, effectuation, and bricolage is about understanding the degrees of freedom available to the innovation team. Under causation, there is a sense that both means and outcomes (implying a successful market connection to such outcomes) can be controlled. In effectuation, there is recognition that means can be controlled, but the outcomes, in terms of market appeal, are unknown and subject to testing, experimentation, adjustment, reboot, pivot, and so on. In bricolage, there is recognition of the killer product, service, or app that will turn the market on its head, but no clear understanding of how to make that vision come true. So the right technique must fit with the right circumstances, right team, right resources, and so on. Generally, firms that are rife with engineers and research labs lend themselves more readily to effectuation processes, whereas market-based firms better connected with market needs are better suited to bricolage. But there must always be room to adapt – reading and adapting to market needs and technological capabilities is at the core of entrepreneurial success.

If we look at space travel, arguably travel to the moon was bricolage inspired by the vision of John F. Kennedy. The Space Shuttle and International Space Station programs were points of effectuation stemming from the space program, and commercial space travel was largely bricolage driven by the XPrize competition.

Time and Predictability

In my research with Oleksiy Osiyevskyy, we found that there are two distinct and highly influential moderators that influence strategic decision-makers when decisions are being made to pursue entrepreneurial actions. The first is time pressure, or urgency to respond. In a nutshell, if the decision-maker or entrepreneur feels that a threat such as a disruptive substitute is not imminent, but nevertheless likely and potentially game-changing, the manager will allocate resources in pursuit of an entrepreneurial opportunity. But once the time pressure passes a certain point, the motivation drops off swiftly. This result is somewhat counterintuitive, so I want to make sure the point and the logic are put across effectively.

Remember Blockbuster Video Entertainment? If you live in North America and are over twenty years old, I don't know how you could not know Blockbuster. It was the undisputed market leader in video rentals, with an impressive network of rental shops across North America. Then along came Reed Hastings, a former math teacher who had already completed one successful tech venture and was just taking life easy when he rented a movie from Blockbuster. Ironically, the movie he rented was Ron Howard's *Apollo 13*. Anyhow, Hastings was late in returning the movie, and having faced a steep late fee, he decided to take on the Blockbuster rental model with a tech-based disruption. If you don't know Netflix's beginnings, you will no doubt know what the firm does today as the leading streaming home video content provider.

Hasting's first model was DVD delivery by mail. It is probable that Blockbuster executives could not contain their laughter when Hastings launched his business. The most respect he received was from analysts who predicted that Netflix could be saved if he sold it to Blockbuster. In the true fashion of a disruption, Netflix was painfully weak in the value propositions of the day – no impulse buying (for you had to wait two days for your DVD to arrive in the mail), limited supply, not necessarily the newest movies, and so on. But what Hastings introduced was a customized recommendation system that helped people find movies they liked instead of taking a risk. He also 100 percent eliminated those nasty late fees.

Blockbuster moved from seeing Netflix as a joke to eliminating late fees (sort of) and eventually to offering home delivery; all the while, it played catch-up to its upstart competitor. The other key distinction was that the original Netflix model was actually designed as an interim model while Hastings prepared the market for online streaming. He was pursuing a customer base, not DVD rentals, and eventually Blockbuster realized that it was weighted down with a major real estate burden that Netflix did not have. This is where the other critical factor, predictability, comes into play. Netflix had a vision of where its future was in a fully home-wired world. Blockbuster did not have that vision. It did not consider the inevitable challenge that few customers would go to a store to rent a movie that was available through a web service. Blockbuster left the door open for our regular closers, Apple (through the Apple TV), to complete the vision and provide predictability.

Incumbent firms are best to move quickly when a disruptive model first threatens their business. Over time, rigidity sets in and managers are blinded by the competition and unable to see the options. They become steadily more defensive of their own model. It is never a good idea to brush aside new competitors prematurely.

Lessons can be learned. If the management team waits too long, it becomes futile to consider change. Instead, like the captain of a sea vessel, the CEO may see that it is time to go down with the ship. Also, incumbents need to move quickly to either adapt an effective effectuation process, or set a bold vision and pursue bricolage as a means to maintain their competitive position. A competitive lead can quickly be lost in today's business world.

Chapter Summary

The main messages in this chapter are:

1 Opportunities are both discovered and created.

2 Opportunity discovery and creation are not the exclusive domain of a few "creative" people, but can be purposefully and
somewhat systematically identified using various frameworks
and tools.

3 An entrepreneurial culture embodies the principles of (1) a clear
narrative of entrepreneurial success within the firm, (2) acceptance of failure, (3) the promoting and rewarding of learning,
and (4) the support of risk-taking as an endeavor, albeit within
limits (i.e., don't bet the farm, at least not with every new idea).

4 Research indicates that effective entrepreneurial action relies
on effectual reasoning or bricolage. Effectual reasoning can best
be described as starting with clear means but unclear goals.
Bricolage is described making do with what you have – it is
a form of "tinkering" to fulfill a vision with what means are
at hand.

5 Urgency can be a strong positive *or* negative influence on
entrepreneurial motivation.

6 Predictability or a sense of confidence in trajectory toward a
clear vision is a positive driver of entrepreneurial intentions.

PART THREE

Entrepreneurial Thinking in Action

8 Dual-Core Processing at Work

Successful innovators are conservative. They have to be. They are not "risk-focused"; they are "opportunity focused."

Peter Drucker[1]

This quote from the great Peter Drucker is short, but also quite deep and telling. To be sure, there is now a body of research and evidence that confirms that the rags-to-riches entrepreneur – or more appropriately, the new venture entrepreneur – does not typically view herself as a risk taker. This is due to two main factors: (1) not having the experience to know better, and (2) an unrelenting belief that the venture is exactly what the market needs and is therefore destined for success. So the above quote may be easy to understand from the perspective of a new venture entrepreneur, but what about the *corporate* entrepreneur?

When a corporation makes entrepreneurial choices, it is replacing something known and previously successful with something unknown, untested, and unreliable. In the corporate setting where entrepreneurship is chosen for either an expansion of corporate scope or a shift of focus, there is definitely risk. Still, Drucker's quote was actually aimed at the corporate entrepreneur at least as much as at the new venture entrepreneur.

I should clarify that Drucker identifies entrepreneurship as a "practice" that encompasses innovative actions. For Drucker, innovation is also a discipline and a practice, and the entrepreneur plays a vital role as the organization's implementer and driver of the strategies associated with successful entrepreneurship. Another favorite Drucker quote of mine is in the preface to *Innovation and Entrepreneurship*, where he says that his book "treats innovation and entrepreneurship, in fact, as part of the executive's job."[2]

Drucker's 1985 book helped launch the study of entrepreneurship as a practice, as opposed to focusing on personality characteristics and risk profiles when defining who an entrepreneur is. His work focused on how business executives can demonstrate sustainability through corporate entrepreneurship. He also saw the need for strategic management within the corporate decision-making infrastructure. Drucker knew that the management academy would eventually understand the complex links between entrepreneurship within existing businesses on the one hand, and the need for strategic management to direct ongoing operations on the other.

Nevertheless, Drucker maintains that the most successful innovators – by which can be meant corporate entrepreneurs – are more opportunity-focused than risk-focused, and this is exactly what I have found in reviewing some of the most successful firms.

In this chapter, I examine some companies that have been entrepreneurial in their growth and development. I then pull together the findings from these observations to illustrate how the elements of entrepreneurial thinking drive strategic entrepreneurship and long-term corporate sustainability. I also include several public sector examples. This should help the reader see how strategic entrepreneurship, and the injection of entrepreneurial thinking, can prepare any organization for changing conditions.

Some Entrepreneurial Thinking Examples

One of the more unique examples of corporate entrepreneurship is the bold drive for sustainability at Interface Global, the world's largest modular carpet manufacturer. A Nasdaq-listed company, Interface started in 1973 with a relatively conventional business model to expand the market for modular carpets, which involves the idea that carpets can be laid in tiles rather than continuous rolls. Modular carpets allow for replacement in heavily worn areas and are often patterned to disguise the introduction of new tiles. Ray Anderson, a chemical engineer with an inclination to innovate, founded Interface.

Modular carpeting was itself innovative, but the power of entrepreneurial thinking and strategic entrepreneurship gripped Anderson more than twenty years after he founded the company. In 1994, spurred largely by customers' questions, his employees asked him to share his environmental vision for the company. Years later, Anderson admitted in a documentary that he did not have an environmental vision for the firm, but he also did not want to let down his employees, so he went to work developing such a vision. His main inspiration was Paul Hawken's book, *The Ecology of Commerce* – in particular, Hawken's phrase, "the death of birth." The moment was, in Anderson's own words, an "epiphany."

Interface embarked on an amazingly bold strategic initiative, called Mission Zero™, which set the long-term goal of eliminating any negative impact the company might have on the environment by the year 2020. Anderson declared that if the goal was not achieved, the company would close its doors. He also stated in a *Fortune* magazine interview, and in the documentary film *The Corporation*, that business leaders who continue to damage the environment will one day be viewed as criminals. For the CEO of a major public company to prioritize environmental sustainability over profitability was completely unheard of.

Predictably, shares in Interface dropped almost immediately. The pressure mounted, for investors were confused about Anderson's new strategy and what it would mean for the firm's long-term viability. But Anderson's faith was based on the synergies between economics and sustainability. He had never accepted the trade-off argument, and as a true entrepreneurial and integrative thinker, he saw that by recycling carpet tiles, he could in fact reduce the extraction of new materials, protect the environment, reduce costs, improve margins, and expand profits. To better control the circular supply chain, Interface shifted to a lease rather than sale model so that all old carpet tiles were automatically returned as feedstock for the production of new tiles. Not long after declaring Mission Zero, Anderson's team devised a process for producing new carpet tiles of 100% recycled carpet. Interface has continued to expand and continues to lead the industry. Its share price has recovered, and Mission Zero continues to be a goal, now much more within reach. Sadly, Ray Anderson died in 2012, but the drive to Mission Zero continues as a legacy. Here is an excerpt from the company's website:

> What's next? In the future, we hope to not only change our business, but help others to change theirs – beyond the collaborative networks we participate in today. We hope for Interface to become a restorative company, giving back more than we take. We believe in the power of influence to restore both our economy and our environment.[3]

This is a stirring example of entrepreneurial thinking, leading to corporate entrepreneurship, leading to longevity and a legacy, all in the context of clear and purposeful strategic management.

Based on its checkered if not messy history, Nucor Steel was an unlikely candidate to become North America's largest steel manufacturer. As noted in an earlier chapter, Nucor began its corporate existence as an automaker in 1905, founded by Ransom E. Olds. Also as noted earlier, the company filed for bankruptcy protection several times, each time finding the gumption to carry on. Of particular interest to our study is how Nucor has conveyed a somewhat remnant side of its business, mini-mill steel production, to achieve great success.

In 1938, after its first bankruptcy filing, Nucor was forced to abandon the automaking industry. Instead it concentrated on trucks, and ultimately on vehicles for the defence industry. The latter market dried up after the Korean War in 1954, and the company once again found itself insolvent and in need of bankruptcy protection. This time, attractive tax losses made for a battle for control in September 1955. Through a reverse takeover, REO was obliged to take over a tiny company called Nuclear Consultants Inc., changing its name to Nuclear Company of America Inc. The company shortened its name to Nucor and attempted to become a conglomerate (a fashionable move at the time); that included moving its head office from North Carolina to New York, then Phoenix, and finally Florida. It purchased several companies along the way, including Vulcraft Corporation, a steel joist manufacturer. Two great assets came with the Vulcraft purchase – knowledge about and passion for steel manufacturing, and the leadership of Ken Iverson. The rest, as they say, is history – Iverson, working closely with CFO Samuel Siegel, virtually transformed the entire steel industry by adopting, refining, and developing the mini-mill manufacturing process, which ultimately led to Nucor becoming the largest steel manufacturer in North America.

Along the way, Iverson, who had an acute understanding of how commodity-based industries go through cycles, took immense risks, buying companies and plants in downturns and stockpiling cash during strong cycles. Eventually he bought out almost all of his major competitors, and meanwhile, the more affordable mini-mill technology developed to the point that it could produce the highest-quality steel required for the most complex and sophisticated applications. Nucor has since expanded into pre-engineered building systems.

As amazing as that business story is, the true entrepreneurial success of Nucor most probably lies in the culture established by Iverson and carried on to this day. The Nucor culture encompasses five areas: decentralized management, performance-based compensation, egalitarian benefits, customer service and quality, and technological leadership. Unique in the industry is that not one of the Nucor plants or operations is unionized. Decisions are decentralized to ensure local participation and ownership, benefits are provided equally, and compensation systems include performance pay at all levels of the organization. All employees are encouraged to seek out innovative new processes to improve the cost-effectiveness and quality of their products, and they are directly rewarded for their efforts. Nucor's latest innovative pursuit is to become a leader in environmental performance, an announced objective of recently retired CEO, Dan DiMicco. In 2014, John Ferriola, a twenty-year employee, took the helm as chair and CEO of Nucor, pledging to continue the legacy started by Ken Iverson.

An engaging and open organization culture is very common among firms that practice corporate entrepreneurship, but none is more unique than W.L. Gore, the makers of Gore-Tex fabric and various products based on polytetrafluoroethylene (PTFE). Bill Gore founded the company with his wife Genevieve Gore after sixteen years in technical positions, including working with fluoropolymers, at DuPont. Bill and Genevieve's dream was to found an organization that ran democratically, without bosses telling people what to do, but with people self-selecting which projects they wanted to work on, who would be on their team, and so on. The Gores have run their company like a democracy since founding it in 1958, and formalized and adopted their invention of the "lattice organization" in 1967. Like any good scientist, Gore presented his ideas in a paper titled "The Lattice Organization – A Philosophy of Enterprise" and distributed it to Gore associates in 1976. The lattice organization has proven that success can come in a significantly different organizational form. W.L. Gore has been named to *Fortune Magazine*'s US list of 100 Best Companies to Work For since 1984. Associates adhere to four basic principles articulated by Bill Gore, and accessed through the W.L. Gore and Associates website:

- Fairness to each other and everyone with whom we come in contact[4]
- Freedom to encourage, help, and allow other associates to grow in knowledge, skill, and scope of responsibility
- The ability to make one's own commitments and keep them
- Consultation with other associates before undertaking actions that could impact the reputation of the company

It is natural to think that these principles could work for a small team, but W.L. Gore and Associates has reported revenues of $3.2 billion and more than 10,000 employees. The scale of the lattice organization was not conceived at the start, but still it works because the overall scale of each individual operation is restricted to 200 or so people, with more than thirty locations around the world. The company's own materials describe the culture as follows:

> There are no traditional organizational charts, no chains of command, nor predetermined channels of communication. Instead, we communicate directly with each other and are accountable to fellow members of our multi-disciplined teams. We encourage hands-on innovation, involving those closest to a project in decision making. Teams organize around opportunities and leaders emerge.

To be fair, some structure has been added to the organization, including a CEO (selected by the associates) and four major divisions with several product-focused business units. Gary Hamel, a professor at the London Business School and co-founder of Management Information eXchange, has studied the organization extensively and identifies it as "wholly original and endlessly inspirational."[5]

You might wonder how people at W.L. Gore are held accountable for their actions. Duties are negotiated with team members, and commitments are made that are taken as sacred oaths. Each year, associates are evaluated by twenty to thirty of their peers, and in turn each associate must evaluate twenty to thirty peers. Each employee is forced to rank those they evaluate from top to bottom; then select cross-functional committees discuss the results and develop overall rankings from 1 to 20. Compensation is based on these evaluations. Leadership positions are earned through "natural" leadership. All associates are owners in the privately held company.

This organizational culture and system has driven W.L. Gore and Associates to be a highly prolific innovator of myriad products (around 1,000), most of which have their roots in the core technology of PTFE. They include Gore-Tex, medical devices (synthetic blood vessels), guitar strings, and diverse industrial products, including the structural materials that were used in the retractable roof at Wimbledon.

Gore is not the norm, but like 3M, it is an aspirational example of a truly entrepreneurial yet strategic, large, and growing organization. 3M and Nucor are both more than 100 years old, and Gore is more than 55 years old, and all three are still entrepreneurial and growing.

3M has often been recognized as one of the most innovative firms of our time. The history of 3M is well documented in its 2002 publication, "A Century of Innovation: The 3M Story."[6] In a way, it seems trite to include a company like 3M, because it is not exactly a typical company – it is known for innovation, and hence one would presume that it is an entrepreneurial firm. Still, it is instructive to understand what makes 3M entrepreneurial.

One element that stands out is its constant research and experimentation to find new materials and new products; this is matched with the need to fit the new materials to product opportunities. This is not always easy to do and has resulted in 3M having a widely diverse customer base. It must also be said that a company with 3M's reputation can become a self-fulfilled prophecy: people who long to be innovators will be attracted to such a firm.

In describing its culture, 3M states that it has a "tolerance for tinkering," driven largely by the 15 percent rule, which means that employees are encouraged to use 15 percent of their time to do whatever they want. The firm's 100-year celebration was summarized as a series of statements known as "time-tested truths." Table 8.1 links some of these truths to the elements of entrepreneurial thinking described in the previous chapter. These statements, and many more on the full list, speak to opportunity discovery or creation, the need for strong entrepreneurial culture, and the ability and commitment to follow through on innovative initiatives, which are the three core tenets of entrepreneurial thinking.

Another example of longevity by strategic entrepreneurship is IBM. IBM was formed through the merger of three firms in 1911 and

Table 8.1 Entrepreneurial thinking and a selection of 3M's "time-tested truths"

3M time-tested truths	Entrepreneurial thinking
Give good people opportunities, support them and watch them thrive.	A belief that opportunities can be discovered or created.
"White spaces" are the untapped markets with promise that 3M has not yet entered.	
Innovation flourishes in diverse small groups of committed people.	A belief that an entrepreneur-driven culture drives exploration.
The most successful innovators network, interact, and share their knowledge – and problems.	
Collaborate early and often.	
It's difficult to succeed alone; building a career at 3M requires the support of others.	
The most successful 3M leaders have been mentors, sponsors, champions – or all three.	
At their best, 3M divisions are entrepreneurial and focus on their customers.	
Conceive, believe, achieve. Persistence – combined with creativity and faith – is still the best formula for long-term success.	A belief in the ability to achieve entrepreneurial outcomes through action.
It's not up to 3M's customers to ask for products they need; it's up to the company to anticipate the needs customers don't even know they have and develop product solutions.	
"Patient money" and patient people help the big ideas generate.	
Consistent, long-term investment in R&D is crucial to innovation success.	
Be open to ideas from unexpected quarters.	Growth mindset.
Don't let one approach or solution blind you to better options.	
Struggle is a necessary component of success.	Iterative trajectory of ideas.
Innovation comes from individual initiative not just following orders.	
3M's strategy is global, but it's implementation is local.	Local and distant search.
Randomness and chaos are both part of innovation.	Business planning based on the belief foundation of trial and error.
A "loose-tight" philosophy of management balances entrepreneurial action and corporate consistency where it matters most.	The basis of strategic entrepreneurship.

was originally called the Computing Tabulating Recording (CTR) Company. CTR manufactured a wide range of products, including employee time-keeping equipment, weighing scales, automatic meat slicers, coffee grinders, and punch-card equipment. From this frontier, IBM went through at least five major entrepreneurial-driven shifts:

1 In 1915, new leader Thomas Watson Sr. instituted many corporate culture innovations, such as employee education and employee sports teams, in the belief that well-supported employees foster a healthy and effective workplace. Watson also renamed CTR as International Business Machines and created the slogan "THINK."

2 During the Great Depression of the 1930s, IBM expanded and "bet the company" by continuing to manufacture a huge inventory of tabulating equipment, which positioned the firm to take on government contracts.

3 In the late 1950s, Thomas Watson Jr. boldly stated that "it shall be the policy of IBM to use solid-state circuitry in all machine developments. Furthermore, no new commercial machines or devices shall be announced which make primary use of tube circuitry."[7] This was a truly rare and bold initiative by a CEO: he was declaring the adoption of disruptive technology. This bold move led to the "golden decade" of the 1960s, when IBM dominated the early years of the computing industry.

4 In 1981, IBM again shifted dramatically, from claiming that personal computers would not overcome mainframe computers, to instead taking a leadership position in the fledgling PC industry. Another entrepreneurial move was to abandon the standard vertical integration of computer components to allow Microsoft to supply the operating system, and Intel the microprocessors.

5 In 1995, new leader Lou Gerstner followed previous IBM bold moves by abandoning the PC industry and creationg a new integrator role of technology management, hardware, software development, and consulting.

In many ways, IBM is the poster corporation for strategic entrepreneurship: at that firm, the stability of strategic management is constantly monitored with entrepreneurial thinking, and this positions the firm to engage corporate entrepreneurship periodically to pierce through the stable path and to jolt the organization onto a new trajectory. Of particular note is that IBM had utterly rejected the PC before 1981. However, it monitored the situation closely, and as reported by Peter Drucker in his 1985 book *Innovation and Entrepreneurship*, when IBM witnessed the enthusiasm of young people playing games on early personal computers, it quickly established a task force and developed the IBM PC, which was superior to all competitors. This is clear evidence of opportunity seeking. IBM's culture was open to a growth mindset as well as to experimentation, and it was confident of being able to follow through on its entrepreneurial initiatives.

DuPont is another long-term survivor that went through significant shifts: from gunpowder manufacturing, to dynamite, to polymers (most notably, nylon), to Tyvek and Corian, and more recently to the production of agriculture products. DuPont was formed in 1802, which means it is the oldest company included in the Dow Jones 30 index. For over 100 years, DuPont focused on gunpowder and dynamite; then it was forced to diversify to address anti-trust directives. This led the firm to become one of the great research-oriented entrepreneurial firms of all time.

It is important to also consider examples of corporate entrepreneurship in the public sector. I will share two examples, both of which are local and both of which are well known to me personally.

I live in Calgary, a western Canadian city of approximately 1.3 million people. Unlike in other cities, there is only one public school board, which makes the Calgary Board of Education one of the largest in Canada, with over 110,000 students. It is difficult for such a large and diverse board to manage the changing demographics and life cycle changes in communities. Also, because of the single-board system and a highly affluent citizenship, private schools are plentiful (and expanding). The public board does not want to lose its best students to private schools, so there is significant pressure to effectively allocate resources and make sure all school properties are delivering at a high level.

Central Memorial High School had been built to serve the children of an affluent neighborhood in southwest Calgary. Over time, the school encountered difficulty sustaining its student body, and school board officials wondered whether it was the best use of taxpayer funds to continue to offer high school programming there. They asked an innovative principal, Jeff Turner, to take on the leadership of the school and consider options for increasing its attractiveness for students.

Jeff asked his new department heads for ideas. It did not take long for Jeff, who was very supportive of the arts, to develop an idea with the Fine Arts department head, Bob Chudyk, that would see the school focusing on the performing arts. The school had long offered a strong fine arts program, but the proposal required a rethink to accommodate expansion, including new hires and the renovation of classrooms to accommodate the new initiative. But it was creative and new, so Jeff thought, *Why not?*

After myriad trials and tribulations both within and outside the school, the program was highly successful; it even attracted significant numbers of students from private schools. As an unexpected bonus, the new curriculum even had an impact on a significant number of academic components of the school, injecting the energy and creativity of the performing arts into social studies, maths, sciences, and so on. A telling sign of this success is that the school administration required additional resources, not for the program, but to address the flood of inquiries from other schools, school boards, administrations, and so on. When Jeff and Bob were asked why the program worked, they identified four key elements:

1 *Political support* from the local trustee, Nancy Close. There were constant resource battles, and the standard challenges relating to prioritization of the 3R's (today they would likely be "STEM" battles), so political support was critical in moving the program across the line.

2 *Middle-management leadership.* Jeff and Bob both played important roles. Jeff, as head of the entire school, showed unwavering
support for the performing arts initiative. Bob was responsible
for making it work – biannual performances in dance, music,
theater, musical theater, and visual arts were critical to the venture, which meant that all manner of spaces had to be converted
into dance studios, technical stages, and so on.

3 *Organizational culture.* Initially, the academic components of
the school did not quite buy into this new focus, but after the
other staff observed the energy and enthusiasm of the students,
performing arts found its way into other subjects, and examples
from those programs were used to explain topics in English,
maths, and sciences.

4 *Long-term perspective.* Right from the start, sustainability was
critical to both Jeff and Bob. They knew that the program could
not rely on them personally and that the change had to be self-
sustainable. To promote sustainability, they instituted a four-
point plan:

  (a) A clear vision statement embracing the entire school (including
short- and long-term measurable goals for the whole school).

  (b) Hiring the right people with the right skill sets and passion
(and working closely with those who were not as passionate
to help them find attractive options, recognizing the union
environment).

  (c) Holding the entire team to high standards (and achieving
the goals).

  (d) Empowering individuals to create their own areas of excellence (especially outside the Fine Arts department) as part of
creating a culture of excellence.

The school continues to attract top academic and creative students,
even though both Jeff and Bob have since retired. This is a mark of
entrepreneurial success – long-term sustainability and growth.

How the Central Memorial High School story evolved reflects a
series of health care innovations in the late 1990s. I was fortunate to

be a junior member of a research team, funded by the Alberta provincial government, that studied innovations in the public health care system. Many of the studies from this period were published, and I was fortunate to be a co-author on a study of how dynamic capabilities could be identified, enabled, and managed through innovation. "Dynamic capabilities" is an academic term for managerial capabilities; it draws on organizational, financial, and human resources and competencies to reshape those resources and competencies to enhance the organization's ability to adapt to a changing environment. In this sense, there is a direct link between dynamic capabilities and entrepreneurial thinking: both are enactment processes for driving entrepreneurship within an organization. Dynamic capabilities is a more generic term that reflects various forms of engagement, whereas entrepreneurial thinking follows a specific platform grounded in cognitive psychology and motivation theory.

Our study focused on the introduction of interdisciplinary primary health care clinics as an alternative to traditional delivery. It was published in one of the top management journals, *Journal of Management Studies*.[8] In our study, we identified three principal stages through which corporate entrepreneurship can be implemented in the public sector:

1 Identify latent dynamic capabilities within the organization. Translated – identify how new knowledge has been historically created within the field of focus. In health care it was through controlled experimentation, which would be familiar to medical professionals whether through their education or by working with colleagues. In the performing arts field, it was through preparing and engaging in performances – putting to the test the ability to raise the curtain on opening night.
2 Enabling dynamic capabilities requires two sub-stages: (1) creating opportunities for individuals to take personal initiative, and (2) encouraging the development of teams and trusting relationships. Both these sub-stages, which reflect truths/beliefs from 3M and Gore, were evident in both the health care and performing arts examples.

3 Middle management plays an important role in balancing the
tensions between front-line workers who take individual initiative, and organizational needs for guidance and control.

What is interesting and illustrative about these two examples is
that they identify how non-entrepreneurial organizations – and,
let's be frank, organizations that have no interest in being entrepreneurial – can still be a home for entrepreneurial activities. Our study
described how entrepreneurial actions can take hold even within
seemingly non-entrepreneurial organizations, through the adoption
of a three-stage approach: (1) identify innovative processes that may
be latent but are nevertheless familiar to employees (identified here
as dynamic capabilities); (2) enable the enactment of these capabilities through individual initiative and team support; and (3) continuously manage the local–central tension.

Earlier, I commented on two other highly entrepreneurial firms
that are local to Calgary; R&P and First Energy. Many other companies I know personally have engaged in entrepreneurial thinking on
a recurring basis, and much of it has generated tremendous results
in innovation and corporate entrepreneurship. Here are a few more
examples:

- PHX Energy Services Corp. is a global horizontal- and direction-
  drilling company, founded by John Hooks. I had the pleasure
  of interviewing John, who is a steadfast believer in the power of
  corporate entrepreneurship and innovation to drive corporate
  culture, success, and longevity. Recently, the R&D team was
  asked to address a problem of communicating drilling information, which is typically done through electro-magnetic devices,
  when the formations are non-conductive and hence unable to
  transmit data. The transmission tool developed at PHX was
  enhanced to meet the challenge, and this provided a unique
  advantage over its competitors.
- In the energy sector, many firms have expanded through "fracking" and *in situ* development of the Alberta Oil Sands. Fracking, a
  technology developed in Canada, is changing resource capabilities

globally, most notably in the United States. Investment in the oil sands is over $500 billion, some of it by huge multinationals such as Exxon and Shell. Independent Canadian energy companies took the entrepreneurial risk of investing in this high-risk, long-term, big investment opportunity, led by Murray Edwards, a significant shareholder and key strategist for CNRL.

- Another industry that is typically reserved for only the largest of corporations is downtown office construction. Institutional investors include the Canadian Pension Plan Investment Board (CPPIB), the Ontario Teachers' Pension Plan (OTPP), the British Columbia Investment Management Corporation (bcIMC), and the Alberta Investment Management Corporation (AIMCo). Two private companies in Calgary have applied entrepreneurial thinking and launched bold initiatives by building the 2 million-square-foot Eighth Avenue Place (Matco Investments Ltd., led by Ron Mathison) and Palliser South (Aspen Properties Ltd., led by Scott Hutcheson).

- Mike Culbert is the CEO of Progress Energy Canada, a pioneer in natural gas exploration and production. He recognized that the future lay in exporting abundant reserves to energy-hungry parts of Asia. This entrepreneurial spirit led to working with Petronas, the national oil company of Malaysia, and to the securing of property rights to build North America's first natural gas liquefaction and export port.

- Bill Borger's family construction business has roots going back almost 100 years. The firm has grown through various corporate entrepreneurial initiatives (vertical and horizontal expansion), and strives to engage each and every employee in the Borger Innovation Coin Game. Although only a few years old, the game offers a coin as a reward for each innovative idea. Over half the employees have earned the stylish coin, which features the firm's core values (Integrity–Safety–Respect–People–Innovation–Teamwork–Collaboration). In the wake of the 2015 Borger Innovation Fair, forty-five new innovations were adopted for practice, and four new patents were applied for.

These examples demonstrate the power of leveraging a corporate platform that features an entrepreneurial culture. I have compiled these examples against the core elements of entrepreneurial thinking motivation theory (from the last chapter) in Table 8.2, to indicate more clearly the importance of combining the resource strengths embedded in existing firms with the power of entrepreneurial thinking.

There are a few interesting connections illustrated in Table 8.2. First, I included two columns for leadership (vision and implementation). Based on the theory and the examples provided, leadership is important, in terms of both pre-entrepreneurship visioning and post-vision implementation. What we see in the chart, which is no surprise, is a clear alignment between situations where firms adopted bricolage as a means to moving forward, and the critical importance of visionary leadership. Powerful examples include Ray Anderson's impassioned vision for saving the planet, Ken Iverson's and Bill and Genevieve's commitment to fairness and inclusion among their teams, and the steadfast determination of the Watsons senior and junior as they led IBM in dramatic corporate entrepreneurship transformations.

In contrast, we see strong links among effectuation and research, experimentation, tinkering, and so on as key drivers of culture. 3M's famous 15 percent rule, Gore's 10 percent dabbling, DuPont's early research orientation, Alberta Health Service's learning by experimenting, and the Borger innovation game all drove cultures and corporate entrepreneurship grounded in effectual reasoning.

Overall, there is evidence of the pulling nature of a powerful vision to drive bricolage, as well as the driving push of research orientation and creativity to drive effectuation processes. There is also a bit of complexity where both processes thrive in unique situations such as Gore (the vision of a democratic organization drove bricolage for organizational innovation, while "dabbling" drove product-focused entrepreneurship), Alberta Health (where senior level visioning drove the establishment of localized effectuation processes grounded in experimentation), and Borger (where senior leadership expanded vertically into participating in the ownership of client projects, while

Table 8.2 Examples mapped against the core elements of entrepreneurial thinking

Company/ situation	Description	Opportunity seeking	Key drivers of culture	Emphasized process	Leadership (vision)	Leadership (implement)
3M	Product innovations	Seek new markets	"Tinkerers," 15% rule	Effectuation	Not as important	Market driven
Interface	Pursue sustainability	Save the lanet	Save the planet	Bricolage	Critical	Critical, persistence
Nucor	Prune to mini-mills	Profitability	Team focus	Bricolage	Critical	Yes, team and shared benefit
Gore	Org. and product innovations	"Lattice" organization	"eable," peer	Bricolage and effectuation	Critical (all levels)	No bosses
IBM1 (1915)	Corporate culture	Employee loyalty	Essence of innovation	Bricolage	Critical	Critical
IBM2 (1935)	Expand in depression	Government work	Expand benefits	Bricolage	Critical	Critical
IBM3 (1957)	Solid-state circuitry	Transform core tech.	Speak Up!	Bricolage	Critical	Critical
IBM4 (1981)	Personal computer	PC growth	Market shift	Bricolage	Critical	Less important
IBM5 (1994)	Shift to tech. integration	Unique new concept	Research oriented	Bricolage	Critical	Less important

DuPont1 (1920s/30s)	Dynamite to polymers	Anti-trust	Research oriented	Effectuation	Not as critical	Questionable
DuPont2 (1960s)	From nylon to Mylar	Continued research	Research, markets	Effectuation	Not as critical	Questionable (diversification)
DuPont3 (2000s)	From Product to agriculture	Continued research	Research focus	Bricolage	Critical	Less important
Alberta Health	Primary care clinic	Better-quality care	Learn by experiment	Bricolage & effectuation	Senior level important	Mid-level important
Central Memorial	Performing Arts program	Save the school	Specialized school	Bricolage	Senior level important	Mid-level important
PHX Tech	R&D	Technology	Prioritize R&D	Effectuation	Senior level important	Mid-level important
CNRL	Heavy oil	National investment	Boldness	Bricolage	Senior level critical	Critical
Matco	Class AA office	Long-term investment	Market knowledge	Bricolage	Senior level critical	Important
Aspen	Class A office	Build capabilities	Growth	Bricolage	Senior level critical	Critical
Progress	LNG Port	Market control	Relations	Bricolage	Senior level critical	Important
Borger	Expansion and culture	Innovation competitions	Inclusive	Effectuation	Important	Critical

driving process innovation by inclusively engaging all employees). This is further evidence that there is far more than a one-best way to drive entrepreneurial thinking, innovation, and corporate entrepreneurship. At the core, firms are most effective when either visionary leadership and bricolage processes create a compelling end goal that *pulls* the organization, or when organizational focus and resource dedication drive them to *push* innovation through effectuation processes such as experimentation, dabbling, and tinkering.

Chapter Summary

The main messages in this chapter are:

1 Entrepreneurial thinking is operationalized in many ways – here are some specific ways:
   (a) Opportunity discovery and creation are systematically developed using techniques such as the strategy canvas and effective brainstorming.
   (b) Organizational culture requires an acceptance of failure, rewarding effort, experimentation, specific learning, and more than anything positivity.
   (c) The ability to execute is transmitted most effectively through two proven entrepreneurial processes – effectuation and bricolage.
2 Entrepreneurial thinking is implemented in existing organizations by following these four steps:
   (a) Establish an organizational culture that accepts entrepreneurial initiative.
   (b) Identify your organization's most adaptable path of effectual or bricolage reasoning.
   (c) Engage in opportunity discovery or creation processes, recognizing the need for individual freedom and team development.
   (d) Support middle management in managing the tension between individual initiative and freedom and organizational guidance and control.

9 Barriers to Success

Progress is a nice word we like to use. But change is its motivator. And change has its enemies.

Robert Kennedy[1]

The reality is stark and worth noting carefully: most entrepreneurial initiatives fail. This is strongly evident in the research on firm failures noted in chapter 2, and equally if not more evident in corporate entrepreneurship. Still, given that failure will eventually overtake the firm that does *not* pursue corporate entrepreneurship, it is best to try, even while recognizing the barriers and pitfalls of entrepreneurial action.

The Advanced Institute of Management Research (AIM Research) is a UK institute of more than 250 fellows and scholars dedicated to developing world-class management research. In a 2008 publication titled *Radical Innovation: Making the Right Bets*,[2] the authors identified twelve "excuses" for rejecting radical innovation projects:

- "It's not our business." This camp might concede that the initiative is interesting, but then goes on to add that it is too far from the organization's core to be worthy of investment. Many firms have missed the next evolution of their industry as a result of this argument, including Encyclopedia Britannica, which did not pursue multimedia CDs and the Internet. Clayton Christensen offers many examples, such as the manufacturer of gasoline-powered cable shovels that failed to adopt hydraulics.

- "It's not a business." That is, a firm fails to see the idea as a business. This is a common excuse for not investing in new technology ventures such as Facebook and Twitter ("How do they make money?"). Possibly the most dramatic "not a business" example was Fred Smith's term paper proposing overnight delivery service, which his professor graded as an unworkable idea. Fred Smith founded Fed-Ex.
- "It's not big enough for us." Large, successful companies struggle with this excuse every day. AIM Research notes that at one point Procter & Gamble sought to create a new business the size of Starbucks each year, which made it difficult to consider smaller ideas, even if they were strong ideas.
- "It wasn't invented here." Pride of authorship can be an important criterion, especially for large, established businesses. A little-discussed lever of Steve Jobs's success at Apple was that he would seek ideas from outside that could be polished and shaped to meet the Apple standard. iTunes, the iPod, and several other groundbreaking products started as ideas/products created by others, then discovered and purchased by Jobs.
- "It was invented here." This is related to the previous excuse – a firm will at times reject an interesting idea developed in-house because it is perceived as inferior to its premium product (noted earlier as a consequence of premium position captivity).
- "We're not cannibals." Sony Music reportedly had the technology and ability to develop iTunes and the iPod well ahead of Apple, but this would have resulted in massive cannibalization of CD sales.
- "It ain't broke so why fix it?" This is a powerful excuse within organizations, and no doubt the dominant reason why firms do not pursue entrepreneurial initiatives. A cautionary note – I don't want readers to think that all innovations or entrepreneurial initiatives are good. Often it is sound to not break what ain't broke. There isn't a clear rule here – judgment is required.

- "Great minds think alike." This excuse is an enactment of group-think. Organizations full of "yes" people, who blindly go along with whatever the boss wants, are super-susceptible to the excuse of great minds thinking alike. Effective leaders always ensure that descending views are welcome and considered.
- "(Existing) customers won't/don't want it." Read Christensen's *The Innovator's Dilemma*, and learn how innovators proceed with great ideas even in the face of customer rejection. What a brilliant contribution to the world (Thanks, Clay).
- "We've never done it before." This is a common response made by incumbent firms when new entrants or competitors present an entrepreneurial alternative. When new entrepreneurial initiatives transform an industry, incumbents need to act fast or fall back on the new learning curve.
- "We're doing okay as we are." The Corporate Executive Board (back in chapter 2) refers to this excuse as falling into the "success trap."
- "Let's set up a pilot." This falls into the category of strategic options, which will be discussed later.

The reasons to not proceed are many. To provide a framework or checklist for budding corporate entrepreneurs, I have placed the barriers under three rubrics:

1 Resistance from within the firm.
2 Resistance from within the supply chain.
3 Resistance from the customer.

Resistance from within the Firm

The most significant hurdle by far is resistance to change from within.

It is fashionable today to have management committees, at various organizational levels, working as teams. Teams can be entrepreneurial, but they first need to function effectively. Patrick Lencioni's

The Five Dysfunctions of a Team: A Leadership Fable[3] highlights the need for teams to confront five fears or concerns:

- *A lack of trust* – team members must learn to trust the intentions and actions of their fellow team members.
- *The fear of confrontation* – team members must learn to be open in communications, and accept conflict as a component of addressing difficult issues and finding effective solutions.
- *The absence of commitment* – team members must be committed to the team, not to their own personal agenda.
- *The absence of accountability* – team members must be held accountable, and hold one another accountable to perform.
- *Failure to focus on goals* – the team members must focus on organizational goals over individual or specific department goals.

Lencioni's book captures the essence of each of the five dysfunctions, allowing the reader to assess how each dysfunction can creep into her organization. All too often, I observe teams that would not be classified as dysfunctional by the team members, but that do not engage in open and honest debate. The outcome is often a "one no" policy – that is, ideas are given to the team members (in the worst case by e-mail), and if one team member has a negative reaction, the idea is scrapped. Leaders tend to feel that they are being consultative and open, but new ideas by their nature require new paths. So it is rarely a straightforward process, and if the team is committed to the goals and direction of the entire organization, one no is an inappropriate test of the idea. Teams are meant to work collaboratively, which means they need to walk through, debate, and likely reshape the idea before making a call.

The research by Kim and Mauborgne,[4] the originators of the Blue Ocean Strategy, on organizational effectiveness in initiating new ideas is very helpful. They outline the four hurdles that need to be leapt for organizational change: (1) the cognitive hurdle, (2) the resource hurdle, (3) the motivational hurdle, and (4) the political hurdle. Kim and Mauborgne name their framework Tipping Point

Leadership, which is slightly confusing, as the term was also popularized by Malcolm Gladwell in his breakout best-seller *The Tipping Point: How Little Things Can Make a Difference.* Curiously, even though Kim and Mauborgne's article was published in 2003, they do not even mention Gladwell's 2000 book of virtually the same name.

Visiting Gladwell's website (Gladwell.com), we find that he describes the tipping point as "that magic moment when an idea, trend, or social behavior crosses a threshold, tips, and spreads like wildfire. Just as a single sick person can start an epidemic of the flu, so too can a small but precisely targeted push cause a fashion trend, the popularity of a new product, or a drop in the crime rate."[5]

Kim and Mauborgne write that "the theory of tipping points, which has its roots in epidemiology, is well known; it hinges on the insight that in any organization, once the beliefs and energies of a critical mass of people are engaged, conversion to a new idea will spread like an epidemic, bringing about fundamental change very quickly."

The two descriptions are very similar. Even more startling, both Gladwell and Kim and Mauborgne used the transformation of the New York City Police Department, under the leadership of Commissioner Bill Bratton, as their primary example of tipping-point change. Where they differ is that Gladwell conducts a more focused study of the phenomenon: how various agents respond, what brings early adopters to the party, and so on. Kim and Mauborge provide a highly structured framework that incorporates an understanding of the participants only insofar as these perspectives can inform the leader. So I have incorporated the four-hurdle framework from Kim and Mauborgne as the better one for discussing how leaders and managers in organizations can move forward with their entrepreneurial discoveries and creations.

The first hurdle is the cognitive hurdle – cognitive in the sense that team players generally do not see the need for change. This ties largely to vision and to being able to see from 30,000 feet where the organization is heading, where markets are heading, and where technology is heading. The purview of senior management – or, in specialized areas, the perspective of specialists – is grounded in significant analysis and data collection that is impossible to share with all of the team members who are required to participate in backing a new initiative. The cognitive hurdle is simple everyday resistance to change, and there is a library of research on this topic. Practically speaking, what is the leader to do?

To address the cognitive hurdle, Kim and Mauborgne recommend putting the resistor in a face-to-face situation with the pending problem – for instance, face to face with customers who are selecting an entrepreneurial option. They share stories of bank managers being forced to wait in line for tellers, and supervisors being forced to ride in small cars on rough work roads, take public transit, use the firm's products, and so on. They argue that leaders more often than not try to use numbers and forecasts, or threats, to confront resistance to change. These techniques fall flat unless the team members truly understand and have leapt over the cognitive hurdle to change. This can only be accomplished by putting the person face to face with the problem and finding creative ways for them to see the challenge from the customer's eyes.

The second hurdle is the resource hurdle, which is resolved by resetting priorities. This requires committed leadership from above, available slack or unused resources, or the ability to reallocate or trade resources. In most cases, the resource hurdle requires finding a way to fund a new initiative – reach a tipping point – without extra resources. Kim and Mauborgne offer many tools for addressing the resource hurdle, including horse trading and hot spotting. Horse trading involves gathering underutilized resources as bargaining chips for trading with other units. With hot spotting, management focuses resources on the areas of greatest need. For instance, Bill Bratton saw the narcotics unit as a priority, so he reallocated funds from other units to get the "hot spot" of narcotics under control – an early win for the NYPD.

The resource hurdle is the essence of Kim and Mauborgne's greatest contribution, the strategy canvas. The strategy canvas is a tool for assessing relative resource concentrations across specific customer factors of choice. Once mapped out, the strategist is tasked with assessing what factors could be reduced or eliminated to generate slack resources that could then be used to raise or create new factors. As an example, when Southwest Airlines introduced point-to-point air travel in Texas, it eliminated reservations, seat assignments, flight food, class distinctions within the flight cabin, and airport lounges; it also reduced the level of airport (Dallas Love instead of Dallas–Fort Worth) and reduced the variety of planes (only 737s), and in the process generated significant resource slack that was re-allocated to the hot spots of frequent flights, lower fares, reliable schedules, and so on. The entrepreneurship of Southwest created a "Blue Ocean," which is Kim and Mauborgne's famous term for an uncontested market space, one that still dominates the airline indus-try some forty years later.

The motivational hurdle moves into another category. No longer is change an idea, or a theory – now it requires change from within. Team members need to be engaged, onside, and active in participat-ing in the change. How do you motivate the team to come onside? Kim and Mauborgne emphasize that broad-brush incentives will not be effective; rather, success lies in identifying the key opinion leaders, engaging them in the change needed, and providing them with a spotlight to illustrate for others the benefits of the change. Working with key influencers to motivate others is one approach, but it requires a thorough understanding of the organization's culture. In the previous chapter, a strong emphasis was placed on establish-ing a culture of openness that encourages initiative and action. In such a culture, the leader must be very careful not to "manipulate" the messaging and instead seek true believers in the entrepreneurial initiative and support their actions. The spotlight should be placed on early adopters and early supporters.

The process of jumping over the motivation hurdle can vary de-pending on whether it is driven primarily by effectuation or brico-lage. As discussed earlier, effectuation is a developmental process led by invention and stepping-stone innovations, whereas bricolage ties more closely to the idea of a compelling end vision, with limited understanding of how the vision will be fulfilled. If entrepreneurship is driven more by effectuation, it is incumbent on the leader to support the champion and seek support from other parts of the organization to help the champion drive forward. With bricolage, motivation lies in finding key influencers, more likely people with legitimate authority throughout the organization, who can bring their sub-teams to see value in pursuing the visionary outcome.

Finally, there is a political hurdle, which can be complex and multidimensional – indeed, the subject of an entirely different book. Put briefly, to pursue corporate entrepreneurship, you need powerful friends from within and often from outside of the organization. Kim and Mauborgne identify three specific strategies:

Angels have the most to gain from the entrepreneurial initiative, so it is critical to build a coalition of angels as early as possible and to keep them apprised and engaged every step of the way. Angels can form an informal advisory council that provides advice to the leader while watching out for naysayers and the development of negative factions within the organization.

Devils are team members who feel they have the most to lose through the entrepreneurial initiative. Note that it is often a *perception* of loss, not necessarily the *reality* of loss. Change is very difficult for many people, and team members often assume a loss through change without having the data or information to support their assessment. The term "devil" is hugely harsh for me personally. Kim and Mauborgne recommend identifying those who feel they will lose, isolating them, understanding their concerns, and addressing them systematically and in isolation from other team members.

Consiglieres are politically adept and respected insiders who can identify land mines and advise a leader on where to focus motivational influence, and possibly resource allocations, to address pending challenges to change.

I like the Kim and Mauborgne framework because the four-level model is simple to remember (cognitive–resource–motivational–political hurdles) yet comprehensive in coverage. It reminds us that entrepreneurship is a team sport and that the entrepreneur –

especially the corporate entrepreneur, because of the entitled nature of an existing work environment, has to engage and enlist the support of as many team members as possible to ensure success.

Getting the Suppliers On Board

Organizations do not operate in isolation, so it is critical to bring key stakeholders, including suppliers and customers, onside with any new initiative. Marshall Fisher of the Wharton School of Business studied the role of suppliers in product innovation and found that it is beneficial to shift suppliers when moving forward with an innovative product. For some, this is sacrilegious, for supplier loyalty is often deeply embedded in a strategic formation of alliances (not just contractual supplier–operator relations). Collaboration can be key to formulating the entrepreneurial initiative, but there is the potential for unintended consequences if the firm does not follow Fisher's advice.[6]

My own experience fits with Fisher's advice. In the late 1990s, I was president and CEO of a master-plan community real estate development company. We conceived the innovation of reconfiguring residential homesites to trade off depth for width, thereby providing a more functional home design, a better streetscape, and better rear yard space. The concept was a full winner except in one particular aspect – it was new and untried, and it changed the conventional industry practice. We were a land development firm, and our business model was to develop residential lots, or homesites (install utilities, roads, etc.), then sell the developed homesites to homebuilders, who were, in a sense, our customers. But to homeowners (the ultimate customers), those homebuilders were co-suppliers. We worked hard to pitch the new lot design to our homebuilder partners, but I don't think they ever got past the idea of designing and building model homes as a favor to our firm. This lack of commitment did much to tank the initiative: customers picked up on the lack of commitment, and this led to slow sales and eventual abandonment of the concept.

How do I know this was a false failure? At the same time that we were struggling with our innovation, a small builder named Mattamy Homes had conceived the exact same idea in central Canada, 2,000 miles from our place of operations. Mattamy decided to integrate all supply operations (in other words, they did both the land development and the homebuilding), which resulted in full commitment to the entrepreneurial venture and innovative product offering. Within a decade, Mattamy had propelled its innovative residential lot and home design until it had become the largest homebuilder in Canada. Supplier commitment was a crucial differentiator between failure and great success. As an interesting aside, almost twenty years later, Mattamy's competitors still refuse to adopt their model (just as airlines still refuse to adopt the Southwest model). I encourage you to go through the twelve excuses and scrutinize your firm's level of excuse making – it is a healthy exercise to undertake.

Fisher presents a simple and logical framework – products vary, as do suppliers. So link innovative products to a "responsive" supply chain, and functional products to an "efficient" supply chain. To address the concerns of the standard supply chain providers, assure them that once developed, the innovative product will be best served by an efficient supply chain, but while in the development stage, responsiveness is essential.

Resistance from the Customer

The customers are in the driver's seat, no doubt about it. They have the luxury of waiting to see what tantalizing offer comes their way, then deciding yeah or nay. In the meantime, the firm and the supply chain invest heavily in the product or service offering, hoping to lure customers. As noted earlier, Christensen's initial "aha" moment was the realization that firms actually abandon some of their best innovations and entrepreneurial initiatives *because* their customers say they don't want them. In this regard, researchers from the City University of Hong Kong found that supplier involvement significantly increases the quality and reliability, time to market, and innovativeness of new products, whereas customer involvement has only a minor influence on quality and reliability.[7]

Customers are firmly in the "prove it to me" camp, and often it is best to seek new customers when pursuing entrepreneurial initiatives and innovative products and services. This is particularly true with disruptive innovations, where product or service features incorporate a new blend that favors different factors (such as the Netflix's no late fees without the convenience of stores on every corner). Even so, it is important to understand the concept of the "liability of newness," a phrase coined by Arthur Stinchcombe to capture the reality that new ideas suffer the most risk of failure when they are first presented, and that the liability lessens over time.

Studies of the liability of newness indicate that customers are less interested in fully understanding the technical benefits of a new product or offering, and instead seek trustworthy support of the initiative. So the corporate entrepreneur must seek ways to build trust and reliance in the offering. This can be done by building alliances of support, having reputable endorsements, establishing high quantity, and using means such as discounts and samples to build a market presence.

In summary, it is important to understand that customer involvement in entrepreneurial initiatives is not necessarily beneficial in improving the offering or in gaining customer support. In fact, Christensen and others have illustrated that there may be devastating unintended consequences of such engagement. It is much better to focus on building trust with the customer through more direct connections to the offering and successful fulfillment.

The Problem with Optionality

Michael Raynor wrote a brilliant book on the paradox of the risk/ reward trade-off, in which he concluded that the best path forward was for leaders to adopt strategic options as a means of consistently testing entrepreneurial initiatives while maintaining a consistent strategic focus for the firm.[8] Theoretically, this is a solid argument, and very much in line with Nassim Nicholas Taleb's recommendation that firms and entrepreneurs pursue optionality as a means of building anti-fragile systems. However, commitment must trump optionality or it will fail.

In the earlier example of my own experience in the real estate development and housing industries, optionality was the kiss of death. Our company offered the optionality of the new residential home and lot, while Mattamy offered no such option – it demonstrated full commitment to its innovation, which removed optionality at the team/employee level. This was compelling to customers, for it built the necessary trust and heartfelt belief to overcome the liability of newness. Also, to avoid the risk of supplier commitment, Mattamy vertically controlled the supply chain by integrating land development and home building operations. Its actions actually eliminated optionality at the supplier level. The message is that, given the choice between a functional reliable product (even at a lower margin) and innovative newness, suppliers, customers, and all other stakeholders (financiers, employees, etc.) will all choose the known option. This is what Fisher was alluding to when he recommended that firms go to new suppliers for innovative product offerings. Optionality is only effective when in full control at a higher corporate level, such as is done in market-base testing.

Optionality is not a risk-averse means of pursuing entrepreneurial initiatives. It can in fact introduce new risks by calling into question the firm's motives, focus, and so on. If used as a means of competing with new offerings, optionality can in fact benefit the new entrant. Consider the introduction of warehouse clubs to retail. Walmart was concerned about Price Club and later Costco because they operate on a business model where product margin is not as important as membership revenues. In other words, they can eliminate the product margin and instead earn profits (now about $2 billion per year) through membership sales alone. Walmart was concerned about the potential disruption this business model presented, so it launched a strategic option called "Sam's Club." It could be argued that the introduction of Sam's Club did not expand Walmart's reach – in fact, it only accounts for approximately one-tenth of corporate sales. But it did provide a sense of legitimacy and recognition for the Costco model. If the almighty Walmart was concerned so much that it was copying the concept, it had to be a good model. Also, because of the labor practices, supply chain arrangements, and other unique elements of the Costco formula, it is hard for Sam's Club to fully imitate Costco; the result is a less effective copycat model that, arguably, boosts Costco and detracts from Walmart's more traditional model.

Optionality is worth considering but is not a surefire path to success. Optionality must be explored in terms of impact on competitors, customers, employees, and suppliers. A comprehensive analysis is essential before pulling the trigger.

Chapter Summary

The main messages in this chapter are:

1 The barriers to corporate entrepreneurship are plentiful and significant in their influence on decision-making. The barriers were considered from three perspectives:
   (a) resistance from within the firm,
   (b) resistance from within the supply chain, and
   (c) resistance from the customer.
2 Resistance from within the firm can be tackled by systematically addressing the four hurdles to change: (1) the cognitive hurdle, (2) the resource hurdle, (3) the motivational hurdle, and (4) the political hurdle.
3 Resistance from within the supply chain may require opting for different suppliers for entrepreneurial initiatives.
4 Resistance from the customer is common and requires vision and trust building.
5 Optionality is not a panacea for risky entrepreneurial venturing. In fact, lack of commitment (which may be the message received through optionality) will often hold back progress.

10 Concluding Comments

To improve is to change, so to be perfect is to have changed often.

Winston Churchill[1]

And so we come to the end of this journey.

What I have tried to demonstrate through this book is that the path to longevity is mired in contradiction when compared to conventional wisdom. For instance, while the conventional wisdom is that we live in fast-changing times, I have argued that we are riding a slow downward wave of exploitation and commoditization, possibly verging on a race to the bottom. Where pundits promote start-ups as being at the core of entrepreneurial transformation, I have argued that corporate entrepreneurship engaging the resources and capabilities of existing organizations is the most effective way to drive progress. Where scholars study sustainable competitive advantage as a path to longevity, I have argued for strategic entrepreneurship, and the need for the firm to be agile and to embrace corporate entrepreneurship and change as a path to longevity. Winston Churchill's words, at the start of this chapter, are instructive – "to improve is to change, so to be perfect is to have changed often."

This book is a call to action – I am asking you to assess your organization and to determine whether you have an organizational culture that will drive innovation and entrepreneurship. Do members of the organization regularly participate in processes aimed at discovering or creating new opportunities? Are innovation and entrepreneurship consciously driven by either visionary bricolage or research-based effectuation? Do you have visionary leadership or implementation-focused leadership to thrust forward new ideas? Does your organization take risks? How do you address resistance to change, whether from within or outside the organization? Let me share what we are doing at our school.

What Are We Doing?

As educators, the priority for my colleagues and I to address is the concern that management research and education is focused too heavily on efficiency over innovation. In response, our business school has taken steps to find a new balance. Specifically, we have launched a core course in entrepreneurial thinking to ensure that important entrepreneurship skills are taught early in a young person's university education. I feel very proud that our faculty and staff have boldly taken on this challenge by adopting the entrepreneurial course as a requirement, not an elective. To receive a degree, each and every student must now learn entrepreneurial thinking as a complement to the critical thinking skills we teach, and students must apply both approaches to active learning initiatives and real-life cases and problems.

Our course is an entirely new experience for students in that it is packed with experiential learning, engages 140 active entrepreneurs and successful business leaders in the classroom, is taught in groups so that students learn how to work in teams (teams selected by us, not them), engages the "flipped"[2] classroom concept, and, most importantly, is capped off with a big-dollar pitch competition (over $100,000 in prizes) to help students learn the importance of communicating their story to investors and stakeholders. I could go on for pages on the energy behind this powerful initiative, which has been truly ground-shaking.

Our entrepreneurship team is led by the first "Teaching" (versus Research) Professorship generated through financial support by RBC Financial, and dedicated to growing entrepreneurs, whether new venture, social, or corporately oriented. We have a blue ribbon donors group and have established the Hunter Centre for Entrepreneurship and Innovation. By the way, first we are transforming the business school, and after that we hope to expand to all corners of the university. The director of the Hunter Centre, who is only two years into a mandate, is developing ways to connect engineers, biologists, medical researchers, environmentalists – indeed, all disciplines – to the power of entrepreneurial thinking, commercialization, and innovation.

Our entrepreneurship core course is one of two disciplinary pillars that are guiding our programming and advancement of our school into the mid-twenty-first century. We have assembled a dream team of academics, coaches, and interdisciplinary leaders to create the Canadian Centre for Advanced Leadership in Business. This center takes all students through a Guided Path System™ to learn about ethical leadership principles at the individual, team, organizational, and societal levels. At each level, we start with a self-assessment, then new learning, followed by experiential practice and journaling/reflection to ensure learning and assessment throughout the program.

I am so very fortunate to be a part of our organization – a tremendous team of dedicated professionals pioneering new ways to ensure that our future generations not only know how to be efficient, but also have the skills to lead change, to seek and create new opportunities to advance our society, and, as a result, to benefit the entrepreneurially focused firms of the future.

Follow us. This is a time for all organizations to set aside resources and to be purposeful and focused in their efforts to promote entrepreneurship, to support entrepreneurial thinking, and to prepare their organizations to pursue longevity through a delicate but essential balance of strategic management and entrepreneurship.

This book is a call-out to corporate leaders, managers, employees, and management students of all ages to pursue longevity with vigor.

The ability of our corporate sector to adapt to paradigm-shifting innovation is unproven at best, and horribly immature at worst (based on the dot.com bubble). The path to longevity and firm sustainability is paved with the skill of entrepreneurial thinking, embracing an entrepreneurial culture, opportunity identification, bricolage, and effectual reasoning. I hope this book will help you find the entrepreneurial spirit and the source of longevity for your organization.

Notes

Introduction

1 I am referring to Institutional Theory, which is a leading theory in organization studies.

2 Many authors have described the impact of commoditization as a "race to the bottom," in the sense that margins continually shrink in the interest of market share and economies of scale. For instance, Kenji Kushida (Stanford University), Jonathan Murray (Innovia Ventures), and John Zysman (UC Berkeley), have argued that cloud computing has resulted in an abundance of capacity, which has caused a shift from "value-based differentiation" to commoditization. The authors refer to this shift as a "race to the bottom" in terms of pricing and profitability. Kushida, Murray, and Zysman, "Cloud Computing: From Scarcity to Abundance," *Journal of Industry, Competition, and Trade* 1 (March 2015), 5–19 at 15.

3 Nassim Nicholas Taleb, *Antifragile: Things That Gain from Disorder* (New York: Random House, 2014), 187.

1 Faster, Smaller, Cheaper: A Time of Great Change?

1 Mark Huberty, "Awaiting the Second Big Data Revolution: From Digital Noise to Value Creation," *Journal of Industry, Competition, and Trade* 15, no. 1 (2015): 35–47. Quote taken from 45.

2 For more information on the term General Purpose Technology, see E. Brynjolfsson and A. McAfee, Research Brief: "Race against the Machine: How the Digital Revolution Is Accelerating Innovation, Driving Productivity, and Irreversibly Transforming Employment and the Economy," MIT Centre for Digital Business, 2012.

3 Ibid., 5.

4 http://www.livescience.com/33749-top-10-inventions-changed-world .html

5 Adapted from Rita McGrath, "The Pace of Technology Adoption Is Speeding Up," HBR Blog Network, *Harvard Business Review*, http:// blogs.hbr.org/2013/11/the-pace-of-technology-adoption-is-speeding- up. McGrath credited her diagram as containing original data from Michael Felton of the *New York Times*.

6 For a description of the electrocution of convict William Kemmler, visit Wikipedia, https://en.wikipedia.org/wiki/War_of_Currents.

7 Thomas Kuhn, *The Structure of Scientific Revolutions* (Chicago: University of Chicago Press, 1962). Kuhn argued that "a paradigm is what members of a scientific community, and they alone, share." My contention is that in terms of business management practice, as a science, a paradigm of exploitation dominated the last half of the twentieth century.

8 See 9.3 in Clayton M. Christensen, *The Innovator's Dilemma: When New Technologies Cause Great Firms to Fail* (Boston: Harvard Business School Press, 1997).

9 This comment is made in reference to Peter Diamandis and Steven Kotler, *Abundance: The Future Is Better than You Think* (New York: The Free Press, 2012).

10 Joseph Schumpeter had a profound impact on economics and manage- ment studies in the twentieth century, although his work is largely misunderstood as providing contrasting views of economic cycles driven by entrepreneurship (Schumpeter I, following the lessons of his 1911 book titled *The Theory of Economic Development*; and Schumpeter II, based on his 1934 book titled *Capitalism, Socialism, and Democracy*). Schumpeter I seems to focus on individual entrepreneurs, while Schumpeter II introduces the corporation as the driver of change and

a new economic cycle. Later in the book I describe how both ideas are actually integrated into one theory.

2 A Delicate Balance: Strategy, Entrepreneurship, and Longevity

1 M.E. Raynor, *The Strategy Paradox: Why Committing to Success Leads to Failure (and What to Do about It)* (New York: Currency Doubleday, 2007).
2 Porter was recently acknowledged as the new Top 50 Thinker; visit http://thinkers50.com/t50-ranking/2015-2.
3 For a thoughtful account of the Red Queen effect in business, refer to Stuart Kauffman, "Escaping the Red Queen Effect," *McKinsey Quarterly* 1 (1995): 118–29.
4 In his recent book *Antifragile: Things That Gain from Disorder*, Nassim Nicholas Taleb espouses the value of tinkering in the form of entrepreneurial bricolage as a means of moving beyond resilience and possibly establishing ways to gain from exogenous volatility.
5 A. Carmeli and G.D. Markman, "Capture, Governance and Resilience: Strategy Implications from the Case of Rome," *Strategic Management Journal* 32(3) (2011): 322–41.

3 The Problem: Firms Fail

1 D.F. Kuratko and D.B. Audretsch, "Strategic Entrepreneurship: Exploring Different Perspectives of an Emerging Concept," *Entrepreneurship Theory and Practice* 33(1) (2009): 1–17 at 5.
2 On 26 January 2014, Senator Rand Paul (Republican – Kentucky), during an interview on CNN's "State of the Union" about President Obama's job creation policy, stated that "what he [President Obama] misunderstands is that nine out of ten businesses fail, so nine out of ten times, he's going to give it to the wrong people." *Bloomberg* and *Forbes* have each published articles indicating that eight out of ten new businesses fail as quickly as within eighteen months.
3 http://www.bls.gov/bdm/us_age_naics_00_table7.txt
4 As reported in the Bureau of Labor Statistics Glossary, http://www.bls.gov/bls/glossary.htm.

5 Hathaway and Litan used firms rather than establishments as their unit of analysis. This resulted in slightly different figures than reported earlier in this chapter from the BLS, including a more rapid failure in the first year of existence.

6 I. Hathaway and R. Litan, "The Other Aging of America: The Increasing Dominance of Older Firms," 8. http://www.brookings.edu/research/papers/2014/07/aging-america-increasing-dominance-older-firms-litan

7 Ibid., 9.

8 M. Olson and D. van Bever, *Stall Points: Most Companies Stop Growing – Yours Doesn't Have To* (New Haven: Yale University Press, 2008).

9 Olson and van Bever, *Stall Points*, 29.

10 I enjoyed reading the terminology used by blogger C. Dixon (http://cdixon.org/2010/01/03/the-next-big-thing-will-start-out-looking-like-a-toy/), who quips that "the next big thing always starts out being dismissed as a 'toy.'"

11 A.S. Grove, *Only the Paranoid Survive* (New York: Doubleday, 1996).

12 Olson and van Bever, *Stall Points*, 86.

4 Longevity: The Capacity to Change

1 Interview: "Lou Gerstner on Corporate Reinvention and Values," *McKinsey Quarterly*, September 2014, 3, conducted by Ian David and Tim Dickinson.

2 R.H. Coase, "The Nature of the Firm," *Economica* (1937): 388.

3 This definition is taken from my own personal notes as an outcome from the 2014 Research Exemplars Conference in Keystone, Colorado, March 2014, co-chaired by Jay Barney and Sharon Alvarez.

4 S.A. Alvarez and J.A. Barney, "Discovery and Creation: Alternative Theories of Entrepreneurial Action," *Strategic Entrepreneurship Journal* 1 (2007): 11–26.

5 M.A. Hitt, R.D. Ireland, D.G. Sirmon, and C.A. Trahms, "Strategic Entrepreneurship: Creating Value for Individuals, Organizations, and Society" *Academy of Management Perspectives* (2011), 58.

6 Adapted from D.A. Whetton and K.S. Cameron, *Developing Management Skills* (8th ed) (Upper Saddle River: Prentice Hall, 2011).

7 R.D. Ireland, M.A. Hitt, S.M. Camp, and D.L. Sexton, *Academy of Management Executive* (2001).

8 J. Dewald and F. Bowen, "Storm Clouds and Silver Linings: Responding to Disruptive Innovations through Cognitive Resilience," *Entrepreneurship, Theory and Practice* 34(1) (2010): 197–218.

9 R. Martin, *Opposable Mind: Winning through Integrative Thinking* (Cambridge, MA: Harvard Business Review Press, 2007).

10 R. Arteaga and J. Hyland, *Pivot: How Top Entrepreneurs Adapt and Change Course to Find Ultimate Success* (New York: Wiley, 2013), 20.

11 Found in Table 2–2 of Christensen and Rayner, *The Innovator's Solution: Creating and Sustaining Successful Growth* (Cambridge, MA: Harvard Business Review Press, 2003). The table is extensive, starting on page 56 and continuing to page 65.

12 For a complete list of the Thinkers50 list for 2013, and a review of the press release that accompanied the revealing of that list, visit http://www.thinkers50.com/wp-content/uploads/Thinkers50_2013_Awards.pdf.

13 In chapter 1, I provide an overview of the framework for invention–innovation–democratization–exploitation modeled on a macro-economic scale.

14 N.J. Foss and J. Lyngsie, "The Emerging Strategic Entrepreneurship Field: Origins, Key Tenets, and Research Gaps" (2011), SMG Working Paper, http://ssm.com/abstract=1747711.

15 Richard Pascale, "The 'Honda Effect' Revisited," *California Management Review* 38(4) (Summer 1996), 84.

16 The description of what ASIMO can do was taken directly from the Honda Corporate website: http://corporate.honda.com/innovation/asimo.aspx, 5 May 2014.

17 Pascale, "The 'Honda Effect' Revisited," 80.

5 Entrepreneurial Thinking and the Human "Dual Core"

1 Richard Rohr, "Daily Meditation," 27 July 2014; adapted from Rohr, *Breathing Under Water: Spirituality and the Twelve Steps* (St Anthony Messenger Press, 2011), 53.

2 Procrastination can be an effective tool for finding the perfect or at least best solution in multi-interest complex situations. But in fact, procrastination is more often used as an avoidance tool. This has been studied in sophisticated detail by Piers Steel, *The Procrastination Equation: How to Stop Putting Things Off and Start Getting Things Done* (New York: HarperCollins, 2011).

3 Graham Allison's *Essence of Decision: Explaining the Cuban Missile Crisis* was published in 1971. After secret information on the proceedings was released, Allison teamed up with Phillip Zelikow for a 1999 updated edition of the book.

4 See Roger Martin, *The Opposable Mind: How Successful Leaders Win through Integrative Thinking* (Cambridge, MA: Harvard Business School Press, 2007).

5 S.A. Alvarez and J.B. Barney, "Discovery and Creation: Alternative Theories of Entrepreneurial Action," *Strategic Entrepreneurship Journal* 1(1–2) (2007): 11–26.

6 C.S. Dweck, *Mindset: The New Psychology of Success* (New York: Ballantine, 2006).

6 The Micro-Foundations of Entrepreneurial Motivation

1 Taken from "Top 32 quotes every entrepreneur should live by," *Forbes*, 2 May 2013, http://www.forbes.com/sites/tanyaprive/2013/05/02/top-32-quotes-every-entrepreneur-should-live-by.

2 K. Guruz, *Higher Education and International Student Mobility in the Global Knowledge Economy* (Albany: SUNY Press, 2011).

3 B. Parsad and L. Lewis (2008). *Distance Education at Degree-Granting Postsecondary Institutions* (Washington: National Center for Educational Statistics, US Department of Education, 2008).

4 Adapted from O. Osiyevskyy and J. Dewald, "Explorative versus Exploitative Business Model Change: The Antecedents of Firm-Level Responses to Disruptive Innovation," *Strategic Entrepreneurship Journal* (2015): 58–78.

5 R.D. Ireland, M.A. Hitt, and D.G. Sirmon, "A Model of Strategic Entrepreneurship: The Construct and Its Dimensions." *Journal of Management* 29 (2003): 963–89.

6 G.G. Dess and G.T. Lumpkin, "The Role of Entrepreneurial Orientation in Stimulating Effective Corporate Entrepreneurship," *Academy of Management Executive* 19 (2005): 147–56.

7 I. Ajzen, "The Theory of Planned Behavior," *Organizational Behavior and Human Decision Processes* 50 (1991): 179–211.

8 Ireland, Hitt, and Sirmon, "A Model," 970.

9 O. Osiyevskyy, L. Hayes, N. Krueger, and C.M. Madill, "Planning to Grow? Exploring the Effect of Business Planning on the Growth of Small and Medium Enterprises (SMEs)," *Entrepreneurial Practice Review* 2(4) (2013): 36–56.

7 Creating the Entrepreneurial Organization

1 This quote is attributed to Peter Drucker. There is some controversy over this: Mark Fields, the president of Ford, attributed the saying to Drucker, but there are some who believe it was Fields himself who said it first.

2 W. Brett Wilson, *Redefining Success: Still Making Mistakes* (Toronto: Penguin Group, 2012).

3 Adapted from Joanne Martin, Martha Feldman, Mary Jo Hatch, and Sim Sitkin, "The Uniqueness Paradox in Organizational Stories," *Administrative Science Quarterly* 28(3) (1983): 438–53.

4 As provided in a presentation to the Haskayne School of Business on 20 October 2014.

5 Jim Whitehurst, *The Open Organization: Igniting Passion and Performance* (Cambridge, MA: Harvard Business Review Press, 2015).

6 Simon Sinek, *Start with Why: How Great Leaders Inspire Everyone to Take Action* (New York: Penguin Group, 2009).

7 Philip Zimbardo and John Boyd, *The Time Paradox: The New Psychology of Time That Will Change Your Life* (New York: Free Press, 2008).

8 Zimbardo and Boyd provided a composite profiling of each of the six perspectives between pages 61 and 65 of *The Time Paradox: The New Psychology of Time That Will Change Your Life*. I have extracted certain key characteristics that I feel effectively transmit each of the perspectives, but I strongly encourage the reader to select and review in detail Zimbardo's extensive work. As the subtitle suggests, it very well may change your life.

9 Findings of the studies of eighteen year subjects were presented in
  Y. Shoda, W. Mischel, and P.K. Peake, "Predicting Adolescent
  Cognitive and Self-Regulatory Competencies from Preschool Delay
  of Gratification," in *Developmental Psychology* 26(2) (1990): 978–86; and
  in a 2007 conference paper, W. Mischel, "Delay of Gratification Ability
  over Time: Mechanisms and Developmental Implications" (2007),
  paper presented at the Association for Psychological Sciences
  Convention in Washington, DC.
10 Zimbardo and Boyd, *The Time Paradox*, 216.
11 Ibid., 297.
12 Fredrickson's research is summarized in *Positivity: Top-Notch Research
  Reveals the 3-to-1 Ratio That Will Change Your Life* (New York: Three
  Rivers Press, 2009).
13 C. Dweck, *Mindset: The New Psychology of Success* (New York:
  Ballantine Books, 2006).
14 Walter Isaacson, *Steve Jobs* (New York: Simon & Schuster, 2011).
15 W. Chan Kim and Renée Mauborgne, *Blue Ocean Strategy: Create
  Uncontested Market Space and Make Competition Irrelevant* (Cambridge,
  MA: Harvard Business Review Press, 2005).
16 C.M. Christensen (2013), http://www.claytonchristensen.com/key-
  concepts.
17 S.D. Sarasvathy, "Causation and Effectuation: Toward a Theoretical
  Shift from Economic Inevitability to Entrepreneurial Contingency,"
  Academy of Management Review 26(2), (2001): 243–63.
18 Claude Lévi-Strauss, *The Savage Mind* (Chicago: University of Chicago
  Press, 1962).
19 The short clip from the 1995 movie *Apollo 13* can be accessed on
  YouTube, https://www.youtube.com/watch?v=C2YZnTL596Q.
  The clip is appropriately titled "Square peg in a round hole."

8 Dual-Core Processing at Work

1 Peter Drucker, *Innovation and Entrepreneurship* (New York: Harper
  & Row, 1985), 140.
2 Ibid., vii.

3 From the Interface website: http://www.interfaceglobal.com/
sustainability/interface-story.aspx.

4 http://www.gore.com/en_xx/aboutus/culture

5 http://www.managementexchange.com/story/
innovation-democracy-wl-gores-original-management-model

6 http://multimedia.3m.com/mws/media/171240O/3m-coi-book-tif
.pdf

7 Emerson W. Pugh, *Building IBM: Shaping and Industry and Its Technology*
(Cambridge, MA: MIT Press, 1995), 230.

8 A.L. Pablo, T. Reay, J.R. Dewald, and A.L. Casebeer, "Identifying,
Enabling, and Managing Dynamic Capabilities in the Public Sector,"
Journal of Management Studies 44(5) (2010): 687–708.

9 Barriers to Success

1 Address by Attorney General Robert F. Kennedy before the US
Conference of Mayors, New York Hilton Hotel, 25 May 1965, http://
www.justice.gov/sites/default/files/ag/legacy/2011/01/20/
05-25-1964.pdf.

2 Written by John Bessant, Kathrin Moslein, Anne-Katrin Neyer, Frank
Piller, and Bettina von Stamm. This and other Executive Briefings are
available at the AIM Research website: AIMresearch.org.

3 Patrick Lencioni, *The Five Dysfunctions of a Team* (San Francisco: Jossey-
Bass, 2002).

4 W. Chan Kim and Renée Mauborgne, "Tipping Point Leadership,"
Harvard Business Review 81(4) (2003): 60–9.

5 http://gladwell.com/the-tipping-point

6 See M.L. Fisher, "What Is the Right Supply Chain for Your Product?"
Harvard Business Review 75(2) (1997): 105–16.

7 H. Sun, H.K. Yau, and E.K.M. Suen, "The Simultaneous Impact of
Supplier and Customer Involvement on New Product Performance,"
Journal of Technology Management and Innovation 5(4) (2010): 70–82.

8 M.E. Raynor, *The Strategy Paradox: Why Committing to Success Leads to
Failure (And What to Do about It)* (New York: Currency Doubleday,
2007).

10 Concluding Comments

1 Winston Churchill, *His Complete Speeches, 1897–1963*, vol. 4, edited by Robert Rhodes James (New York: Chelsea House, 1974), 3706.
2 The "flipped" classroom is aptly named to describe a collection of pedagogical processes used to emphasize learning as opposed to lecturing. The most common adaptation is flipping the lecture and homework – wherein lecture material is provided through videos that students can access at their convenience, and classroom time is used for projects, exercises, discussion, or student presentations.

Index